The Masonic Book Club

Vol. 7A

Masonic Symbols in American Decorative Art

Louis L. Williams & Alphonse Cerza

Westphalia Press
An Imprint of the Policy Studies Organization
Washington, DC

MASONIC SYMBOLS IN AMERICAN DECORATIVE ART

All Rights Reserved © 2025 by Policy Studies Organization

Westphalia Press
An imprint of Policy Studies Organization
1367 Connecticut Avenue NW
Washington, D.C. 20036
info@ipsonet.org

ISBN: 978-1-63723-673-4

Daniel Gutierrez-Sandoval, Executive Director
PSO and Westphalia Press

Updated material and comments on this edition
can be found at the Westphalia Press website:
www.westphaliapress.org

The Masonic Book Club

The *Masonic Book Club* (MBC) was formed in 1970 by two Illinois Masons, Alphonse Cerza, 33°, and Louis L. Williams, 33°. The MBC primarily reprinted out-of-print Masonic books with scholarly introductions; occasionally they would print additional texts as "bonuses" (though none were marked specifically as such on the title pages); sometimes a reprint would be marked "Masonic Book Club Edition"; often an unnumbered bonus was published jointly with the Illinois Lodge of Research or the Supreme Council, 33°, NMJ, USA.

Most of the MBC volumes indicated on the title page, "Volume [*Number*] of the Publications of the Masonic Book Club," some were misnumbered, and some were unnumbered. Indeed, the numbering of the early volumes was inconsistent. For example, *A Serious and Impartial Enquiry* is "Volume Five" (1974) but *Masonic Membership of the Founding Fathers* is "The Masonic Book Club Edition" (1974). Then, *Masonry Dissected* is "Volume Eight" (1977), *The Trestleboard* is "Volume 8A" (1978), and *Anderson's Constitutions of 1738* is "Volume Nine" (1978). If nothing else, MBC books keep bibliophiles on their toes.

The first volumes had deckle-edged paper and pages of slightly different sizes, though eventually the MBC settled into a 6"×9" trimmed-page format for their books. The books were bound in a dark blue fabric with gold lettering. Listed below are the fifty-nine MBC volumes published 1970–2010 with bonuses. N.B.: A number and letter, e.g. "Volume 8A," is a numbering for this reprint series.

The club originally was limited to 333 members, but the number grew to nearly 2,000, with 1,083 members when it dissolved in 2010. In 2017 MW Barry Weer, 33°, the last president of the MBC, transferred the MBC name and assets to the Supreme Council, 33°, SJ, USA. Under the editorship of Arturo de Hoyos, 33°, G∴C∴, and S. Brent Morris, 33°, G∴C∴, the revived Masonic Book Club has the goal of publishing classic Masonic books while supporting Scottish Rite, SJ, USA philanthropies.

Publications of the Masonic Book Club, 1970–2010

1	1970	*The Regius Poem*	Masonic Book Club
2	1971	*The Constitutions of the Free-Masons*	Benjamin Franklin
3	1972	*Ahiman Rezon*	Laurence Dermott
4	1973	*Illustrations of Masonry*	William Preston
5	1974	*A Serious and Impartial Enquiry into the Cause of the Present Decay of Free-Masonry in the Kingdom of Ireland*	Fifield D'Assigny
5A	1974*	*Masonic Membership of the Founding Fathers*	Ronald E. Heaton

6	1975	*The Signers of the Declaration of Independence*	David C. Whitney
7	1976	*The Signers of the Constitution of the United States*	David C. Whitney
7A	1976*	*Masonic Symbols in American Decorative Art*	Louis L. Williams & Alphonse Cerza
8	1977	*Samuel Prichard's Masonry Dissected, 1730*	Harry Carr
8A	1978*	*Trestle-Board (A facsimile of the original Trestle Board by the Baltimore Masonic Convention of 1843)*	Dwight L. Smith
9	1978	*Anderson's Constitutions of 1738*	Lewis Edward & W. J. Hughan
10	1979	*Sufferings of John Coustos*	Wallace McLeod
11	1980	*The Revelations of a Square*	George Oliver
11A	1980	*Biblical Characters in Freemasonry*	John H. Van Gorden
11B	1980*	*A Masonic Reader's Guide*	*Guide* Alphonse Cerza & Thomas Warden
12	1981	*Three Distinct Knocks and Jachin and Boaz*	Harry Carr
13	1982	*Masonic Almanacs and Anti-Masonic Almanacs*	Plez A. Transou
13A	1982*	*Stephen A. Douglas: Freemason*	Wayne C. Temple
14	1983	*The Beginnings of Freemasonry in America*	Melvin M. Johnson
14A	1983*	*Bespangled, Painted & Embroidered: Decorated Masonic Aprons in America, 1790–1850*	Scottish Rite Masonic Museum & Library
14B	1983*	*Making a Mason at Sight*	Louis L. Williams
15	1984	*Masonic Concordance of the Holy Bible*	Charles Clyde Hunt
15A	1984*	*By Square and Compasses: The Building of Lincoln's Home and Its Saga*	Wayne C. Temple

16	1985	*The Old Gothic Constitutions*	Wallace McLeod
16A	1985*	*Modern Historical Characters in Freemasonry*	John H. Van Gorden
17	1986	*The Rise and Development of Organised Freemasonry*	Roy A. Wells
17A	1986*	*Ancient and Early Medieval Historical Characters in Freemasonry*	John H. Van Gorden
18	1987	*The Lodge in Friendship Village and Other Stories*	P. W. George
18A	1987*	*Masonic Charities*	John H. Van Gorden & Stewart M. L. Pollard
18B	1987*	*Medieval Historical Characters in Freemasonry*	John H. Van Gorden
18C	1987*	*George Washington in New York*	Allan Boudreau & Alexander Bleimann
19	1988	*Records of the Hole Crafte and Fellowship of Masons*	Edward Conder, Jr.
20	1989	*A Candid Disquisition of the Principles and Practices of the Most Ancient and Honourable Society of Free and Accepted Masons*	Wellins Calcott
20A	1989*	*Freemasonry and Nauvoo, 1839–1846*	Robin L. Carr
21	1990	*Masonic Odes and Poems*	Rob Morris
22	1991	*Lessing's Masonic Dialogues*	Gotthold Lessing
22A	1991*	*ABC of Freemasonry: A Book for Beginners*	Delmar D. Darrah
23	1992	*The Folger Manuscript*	S. Brent Morris
24	1993	*Freemasonry and Christianity: Lectures from Two Ages*	T. De Witt Peake & John J. Murchison
25	1994	*The Constitutions of St. John's Lodge*	Robin L. Carr
25A	1994*	*The Mystic Tie and Men of Letters*	Robin L. Carr
26	1995	*Recollections of a Masonic Veteran*	S. Brent Morris

27	1996	*The Freemason's Monitor or Illustrations of Masonry in Two Parts*	Thomas Smith Webb
28	1997	*The Masonic Ladder or the Nine Steps to Ancient Freemasonry*	John Sherer
28A	1997*	*Freemasonry and Democracy: Its Evolution in North America*	Allen E. Roberts & Wallace McLeod
29	1998	*The Masonic Harp: Collection of Masonic Odes, Hymns, Songs*	George Wingate Chase
30	1999	*Symbolic Teachings of Masonry and Its Message*	Thomas Milton Stewart
31	2000	*Freemasonry Its Meaning and Significance, An Exposition of its Ethics, Religion and Philosophy*	Otto Caspari
32	2001	*K. R. Cama Masonic Jubilee Volume*	Jivanji Jamshedji Modi
33	2002	*Caementaria Hibernica*	W. J. Chetwode Crawley
34	2003	*A Daily Advancement in Masonic Knowledge*	Wallace McLeod & S. Brent Morris
35	2004	*The Craftsman, and Templar's Textbook and, also, Melodies for the Craft*	Cornelius Moore
36	2005	*The Text Book of Freemasonry*	Retired Member of the Craft
37	2006	*Orations of the Illustrious Brother Frederick Dalcho Esq., M.D.*	Frederick Dalcho
38	2007	*Antiquities of Freemasonry Comprising Illustrations of the Five Grand Periods of Masonry from the Creation of the World to the Dedication of King Solomon's Temple*	George Oliver
39	2008	*Diogenes' Lamp or an Examination of our Present-Day Morality and Enlightenment*	Adam Weishaupt
40	2009	*Proofs of Conspiracy Against All the Governments of Europe*	John Robison
41	2010	*The Evolution of Freemasonry*	Delmar Darrah

* indicates a bonus book

Masonic Symbols in American Decorative Art

MASONIC SYMBOLS IN AMERICAN DECORATIVE ARTS

MASONIC SYMBOLS
IN
AMERICAN DECORATIVE ARTS

VOLUME EIGHT OF THE PUBLICATIONS OF THE MASONIC BOOK CLUB

SCOTTISH RITE MASONIC
MUSEUM OF OUR NATIONAL HERITAGE
LEXINGTON, MASSACHUSETTS

Of 999 copies specially bound for members of The Masonic Book Club, Bloomington, Illinois, this is number

Copyright 1976, Scottish Rite Masonic Museum and Library, Inc.
Library of Congress Catalog Card Number: 76—16690
Printed in the United States of America

Dates of the Exhibition: September 1975 to September 1976

COVER: ALBUM QUILT, cotton applique, Staten Island, N.Y., early 1900's, Museum of Our National Heritage Collection.

PHOTO CREDITS: John Hamilton, Museum of Our National Heritage; Bucks County Historical Society; Corning Glass Museum; Mr. and Mrs. Charles V. Hagler; Henry Ford Museum; Henry Francis du Pont Winterthur Museum; Industrial Color Lab; National Society of the Colonial Dames in the State of Connecticut.

FOREWORD

When the Ancient Accepted Scottish Rite of Freemasons of the Northern Masonic Jurisdiction of the United States of America dedicated its new Museum-Library in Lexington, Massachusetts on April 20, 1975, two hundred years and one day after Paul Revere's ride, it gave an outstanding Bicentennial gift to the people of the United States.

Nestling against a hillside on Massachusetts Avenue, approximately one mile east of the historic Minuteman Statue on Lexington Green, this six million dollar structure is dedicated to the patriotic ideals of the founders of our country. It was built for the express purpose of telling the story of the founding of our United States, of the lofty ideals of those patriots who conceived and brought our Country into being, and of her history down through the years that have followed.

Many of those founders were Masons. Revere, Warren, Hancock, Washington, LaFayette—all carried out in their devotion to this country the high ideals that govern the Masonic Fraternity.

To show how the emblems and symbols used by the Craft were in turn used to decorate the material possessions of the day is the purpose of the exhibit of which this catalog is evidence. It is the first major and inclusive showing of such use by any major Museum anywhere. Thus the Scottish Rite Masonic Museum of Our National Heritage seeks to serve the ideals which animated its builders.

The Masonic Book Club is pleased to be a co-sponsor of the publication of this catalog with the Museum. This catalog is also a first in its field, and will itself become a collector's item as the years go by. So we are happy to place in the hands of our members this unusual Masonic item for your study and pleasure.

LOUIS L. WILLIAMS
ALPHONSE CERZA

CONTENTS

PREFACE	6
INTRODUCTION	9
THE USE OF MASONIC SYMBOLS IN AMERICAN DECORATIVE ARTS	15
GLOSSARY OF SYMBOLS	47
CATALOG	53
BIBLIOGRAPHY	109

PREFACE

Anyone who collects Americana or who has been associated with a history museum is almost certain at one time or another to have come across objects decorated with Masonic symbols. Use of these symbols as a decorative design throughout the 18th and 19th centuries is far more extensive than many people realize. A small number of knowledgeable collectors and dealers has always carefully gathered these unusual decorative art objects and in recent years the number of collectors has grown. Exceptional pieces are commanding rather high prices and even the more common items are becoming more difficult to acquire. These sought-after objects are represented in many art and history museum collections. For the most part, their use in exhibitions has been limited because most curators lack any serious knowledge about Freemasonry or its influence in this country. Consequently, these pieces have been treated either as curiosities or pushed into the darkest recesses of museum storage areas. To be sure, individual items have been duly appreciated or even highly prized. In most instances, however, it is because the specific object is in itself a rarity; the Masonic association is often considered of secondary importance.

We may see that exhibits prepared for the American Bicentennial will include a good number of objects with Masonic symbols. At least one major Bicentennial exhibit, the Boston Museum of Fine Arts' "Paul Revere's Boston," had on display several objects with Masonic symbols, and other museums will probably also note the role of Freemasons in the Revolutionary War.

If Masonic objects have had a limited exposure in museum exhibitions, research on this subject has been almost non-existent. Alan Gowans' important article: "Freemasonry and the Neoclassical Style in America," *Antiques*, February 1960, was one of the first to recognize the influence of Freemasonry and Masonic symbols on American design. The article is by no means comprehensive, but it suggests the need for more serious attention to the subject.

Soon after I became the first director of the Scottish Rite Masonic Museum of Our National Heritage in 1974, it occurred to me that we had a unique opportunity to develop a special study collection of American art objects decorated with Masonic symbols. We already had a nucleus of a collection in the archives of the Supreme Council. I was well aware that these objects also existed in almost every major museum collection, but to my knowledge, no one had ever brought them together in one comprehensive exhibition. When Barbara Franco joined the staff of our new museum in

November, 1974, I placed her in charge of this project. Her M. A. in museum training at the Cooperstown Graduate Programs, and her previous experience as curator of decorative arts at Munson-Williams-Proctor Institute in Utica were perfect qualifications for the assignment.

Almost immediately we initiated an extensive search for information and for significant objects. Our inquiries led us to private collectors, dealers, the Lodges of many Masonic organizations, the key collections of Masonic memorabilia, and several history museums. Particularly helpful in our research were: Roberta Hankamer, Librarian of the Grand Lodge of Most Worshipful Ancient Free and Accepted Masons of the Commonwealth of Massachusetts; Allan Boudreau, Librarian of the Grand Lodge of Free and Accepted Masons of the State of New York; Frank W. Bobb and William A. Carpenter of the Right Worshipful Grand Lodge of the Most Ancient and Honorable Fraternity of Free and Accepted Masons of Pennsylvania; Dr. Silvio Bedini, Deputy Director of the Smithsonian's Museum of History and Technology; Mrs. Dorothy Waterhouse, Waterhouse Wall Hangings, Boston; Susan Finley, National Society of the Colonial Dames of America in the State of Connecticut; Wendy Cooper, Boston Museum of Fine Arts; Olga M. Hughes, Mattatuck Museum, Connecticut; the curatorial and library staff of the Henry Francis du Pont Winterthur Museum; Bucks County Historical Society; and the Museum of the American China Trade.

The numerous lenders to the exhibition are listed in another section of the catalog. I would, however, like to give special thanks to Mr. and Mrs. Charles V. Hagler, Detroit, Michigan, for making available their very substantial collection of objects with Masonic symbols, and for sharing freely with the members of our staff their extensive knowledge and information on this little-known subject.

Publication of this catalog was made possible by a special appropriation of The Supreme Council of the Northern Masonic Jurisdiction of the United States, Stanley F. Maxwell, Sovereign Grand Commander; and a grant from The Masonic Book Club, Bloomington, Illinois. We are grateful to Louis L. Williams, President, who encouraged us in our publication efforts and who rendered valuable editorial assistance; and to Vice President Fred A. Dolan for his guidance and advice on the manufacturing aspects of the catalog.

The catalog was designed by Addis Marshall Osborne, Assistant Director of the Museum of Our National Heritage.

CLEMENT M. SILVESTRO, *Director*

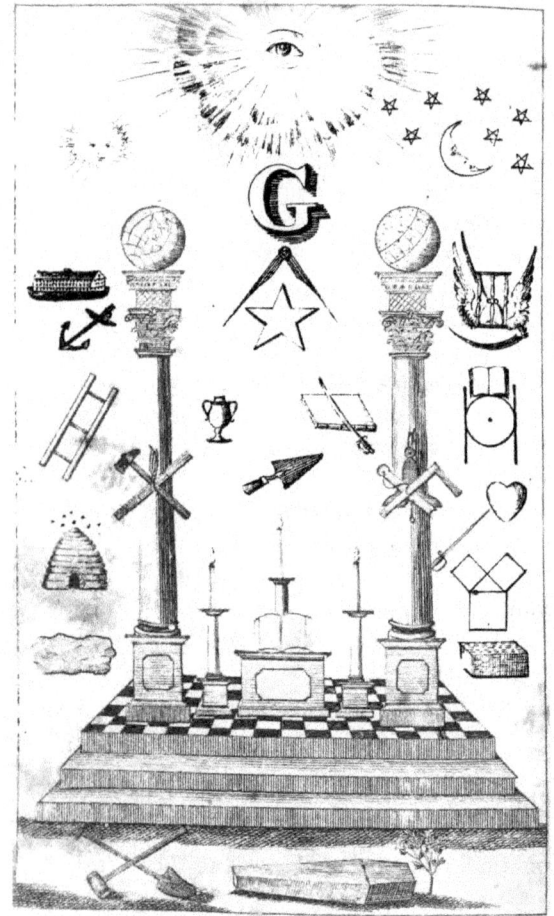

FRONTISPIECE, Jeremy Cross, *Masonic Chart*, 1819, New Haven, Conn. Amos Doolittle, engraver.

INTRODUCTION

A WORD ABOUT FREEMASONRY IN THE UNITED STATES

Freemasonry, as it exists today, is an oath-bound fraternal and benevolent association of men whose purpose is to nurture sound moral and social virtues among its members and all of mankind. Freemasons use the simple tools of the ancient stonemasons—the square and compass, trowel and plumb, among others—as symbols in their teachings. Morality plays, rich in allegory and symbolism, form an important part of their ritual. Belief in a Supreme Being, the Brotherhood of Man, and compassion towards others are primary prerequisites for admission to the Craft. Individuals are not invited to join but must seek membership of their own volition. Character building and brotherly love are the underlying principles of the Freemasons' varied educational endeavors and extensive charitable activities.

Modern Freemasonry had its origins in 17th century England. It was one of several moral and philosophical societies that emerged during the intellectual excitement created by the Newtonian discoveries in science and the general period of "New Learning" stimulated by the Age of Discovery and Exploration. Although Freemasonry's basic philosophical framework is rooted in this age, most scholars agree that its historical antecedents reach back to the medieval craft guilds of operative stonemasons dating from the 14th century. Exact information about their origins remain obscure because of the common practice among societies and associations of the time to keep their proceedings secret, often for political reasons. Early in the 17th century, the once prestigious stonemason guilds—the builders of Europe's great cathedrals—began to accept as honorary members educated gentlemen who were not working masons. These new members were designated "Accepted" Masons (hence the term Free and Accepted Masons). The earliest extant record of the practice dates from 1630 when the London Mason's Company, an organization affiliated with a secret society known as the "Acception," admitted members who were not associated with any building trades. The modern Freemasons freely adapted the tools, implements, and geometrical and

INTRODUCTION

architectural forms associated with operative stonemasons as symbolic images for conveying their moral and philosophical teachings. Mutual protection and assistance, and strong fraternal bonds were also important legacies from the ancient stonemasons.

The movement quickly caught hold and, by the end of the 17th century, "Masonic Lodges" proliferated throughout the British Isles, culminating in 1717 with the organization of the Grand Lodge of England, a central coordinating body with authority to charter subordinate lodges. A Grand Lodge was established in Ireland in 1729 and in Scotland in 1736. All legitimate Masonic lodges throughout the world trace their origin to these three Grand Lodges.

The full flowering of modern Freemasonry occurred in the 18th century and coincided with the period of the Enlightenment, whose unifying characteristic was a faith in the power of reason and the perfectability of man. Perhaps no body of philosophical thought has had a greater impact upon the development of Freemasonry, notwithstanding the fact that the organization was influenced and modified by succeeding philosophical principles in subsequent years. The ideas and ideals of the Age of Reason became integrated with the teachings of Freemasonry. The enduring examples of stonemasonry—the Egyptian pyramids, the Greek and Roman temples, and the Gothic cathedrals—aptly expressed the Enlightenment qualities of Truth, Beauty, Nature and Reason in architectural and mathematical principles. By mid-century Freemasonry had spread to France, the entire European continent, and the American colonies.

Freemasonry's social and fraternal tradition is as important as its philosophical basis. Early Masonic lodges met regularly in coffeehouses and taverns where good food and good spirits made socializing easier and discussion less inhibited. Early records contain numerous accounts of dinners for the membership, a factor that undoubtedly contributed to its growth and popularity. In the American colonies, Masonic lodges continued to meet in taverns and coffeehouses. Punch bowls, flasks, decanters, wine glasses, and china decorated with Masonic symbols became standard service pieces for these festive occasions. Not until the Temperance Movement took root in the mid-19th century, did this convivial dimension of the Craft disappear in the United States.

Freemasonry in the United States has had more extensive application and diversification than in any country in the world. It also has a larger membership than any other nation. Introduced in the American colonies in the early 1730's, it virtually expanded with the nation itself. Boston and Philadelphia each claim the distinction and honor for the establishment of the first legitimate lodges. As early as June, 1731, Benjamin Franklin's *Philadelphia Gazette* contained frequent references to Masonic Lodge meetings held at Tun Tavern in Philadelphia. In July, 1733, Henry Price received a deputation from the Grand Lodge of England to establish a Masonic Lodge in Boston, which met thereafter at the Bunch of Grapes Tavern in King Street. From these two commercial centers Freemasonry spread rapidly and, by the time of the Revolution, it had a firm base in all thirteen colonies.

Individual Freemasons played an important role in the American Revolution, but it would be erroneous to conclude that Freemasons unanimously endorsed the break from the mother country or that the Fraternity acted in unison on political issues of such momentous impact. Several years before the outbreak of hostilities, James Otis spoke against the Crown at the Old First Lodge of Boston, but Masonic Lodges were not seedbeds of revolutionary thought. The one possible exception was St. Andrew's Lodge of Boston, whose members included such prominent patriots as Dr. Joseph Warren, Paul Revere, and John Hancock. Freemasons were found on both sides of the question, but the leadership provided by Masons in this critical period, most notably by George Washington and Benjamin Franklin, is a great source of pride to all American Freemasons. The participation of other important state and local Masonic leaders in the drafting and adoption of the Declaration of Independence, and later of the Constitution, is one of the reasons why Freemasonry today considers patriotism and loyalty to the existing government important underlying principles of its organization.

By the war's end, Masonic Grand Lodges had been established and were flourishing in each of the thirteen original states. Just as the victory at Yorktown had gained Independence for the colonies, the severance of ties with Great Britain also terminated the direct relationship of the American Grand Lodges with the Grand Lodges of England, Ireland and Scotland. Henceforth American Freemasonry would develop independently and would also acquire a distinct character of its own.

The new nation and the new Masonic order virtually grew and developed side by side, a fact that helps to explain the deep-rooted influence the Craft has had in this country. Already firmly established along the Eastern seaboard, Freemasonry quickly moved westward with the popula-

INTRODUCTION

tion. As new territories and states were formed, so were Blue Lodges and Grand Lodges. Quite often Grand Lodges were established in the territories before the states were formed. It was during the years of the early Republic that Masonic symbolism had its greatest influence on the American Decorative Arts and, in fact, American design as a whole.

An unfortunate incident that occurred in Batavia, New York, in 1826, however, interrupted the further expansion of the movement for more than a decade. William Morgan, a Mason of dubious standing, mysteriously disappeared after he had threatened to expose the membership obligations and other Masonic secrets. The Masons of the Finger Lakes area were accused of having cast Morgan into the Niagara rapids and there followed a general reaction against the entire Craft. Protestant ministers were foremost in expressing indignation against Masonry for this unconscionable act. Some scholars have suggested that the incident provided the ministry with an opportunity to attack Freemasonry, which some men of the cloth saw as a threat to established religion. Anti-Masonic excitement forced many lodges in New York and New England to suspend operations, and by 1828, it became an issue in the national elections. A new anti-Masonic political party was formed, and nominated William Wirt for president. By 1832, the anti-Masonic movement seemed to lose its momentum despite continued resentment and agitation against the organization. Andrew Jackson's Masonic affiliation and loyalty (Past Grand Master of the Grand Lodge of Tennessee) failed to obstruct his election as President during the period of anti-Masonic feeling.

Freemasonry's remarkable growth in the United States during the 19th century was aided by the development of an important body of Masonic law and jurisprudence. Much of this Masonic law was incorporated into the constitutions and codes of the Grand Lodges between 1856 and 1875. Nine important works on the subject appeared in this time span. Perhaps the most important code concerned jurisdictional rights, the so-called "American Doctrine," which stated there could be but one Grand Lodge in a state and that no Grand Lodge might invade the territorial sovereignty of another. Codification of their laws and constitutions went a long way toward standardizing the structure and operations of American Freemasonry. Jurisdictional disputes and doctrinal controversies flared occasionally, but by the end of the century, stability and harmony reigned.

Masonic structural organization in the United States is pluralistic and often confusing to members and non-members alike. Three degrees, *En-*

tered *Apprentice, Fellowcraft,* and *Master Mason,* constitute the basic Masonic system known as the Ancient Craft Masonry or, as it is also called, Symbolic or Speculative Masonry. These three degrees are conferred in a Lodge of Ancient Craft Masonry, or "Blue Lodge" as it is popularly known. Local Lodges are under the jurisdiction of the state Grand Lodge.

Beyond the Master Mason degree are higher grades and systems of degrees developed in the 18th century when Freemasonry was still in its formative stages. There are many variations in these higher systems of degrees. In the United States there are two recognized Masonic Rites beyond the basic three degrees of the Blue Lodge. These are the *Ancient and Accepted Scottish Rite* consisting of thirty additional degrees, and the *York* or *American Rite* comprising ten supplementary orders and degrees including the Royal Arch and Knights Templar degrees. One must be a Master Mason of good standing in a Blue Lodge to be affiliated with either of these higher rites.

Today, modern Freemasonry continues to flourish. In the United States membership totals over three and one-half million, and Masonry enjoys a large following in most countries of the world. Freemasonry's ideals, teachings, and benevolent activities continue to have a strong and enduring appeal among men of good will.

CLEMENT M. SILVESTRO
Lexington, Massachusetts

The literature of the subject of Freemasonry is extensive. For this brief summary I have relied upon Henry Wilson Coil's *A Comprehensive View of Freemasonry* (New York, 1954) and Robert J. Lewinski's *What is Freemasonry?* (Silver Springs, Md., 1961). Readers seeking more information should consult Alphonse Cerza's "Masonic Reading List, 1975," *The Philalethes,* Supplement to the February, 1974, issue.

MASONIC MARK JEWEL, silver
Cat. No. 22.

THE USE OF MASONIC SYMBOLS IN
AMERICAN DECORATIVE ARTS

THE USE OF MASONIC SYMBOLS IN AMERICAN DECORATIVE ARTS

The use of Masonic symbols in American decorative arts falls into two main periods. The few examples of colonial objects with Masonic symbols that have survived were almost all related to ritual use in lodges.[1] It was not until American Independence that Masonic symbolism became a significant decorative style in America. From 1775 to 1830 the use of Masonic symbols as decoration occurred with unprecedented frequency. Masonic symbols were used on almost every type of object that was commonly decorated and in almost every material that lent itself to the use of symbols. Examples of utilitarian objects with Masonic decoration from this period include glassware, ceramics, furniture, coverlets, lighting devices, and clocks. The quality of the decoration on Masonic regalia in the period before 1830 is also worthy of serious consideration in the field of American decorative arts. After 1830, the popularity of Masonic symbols abruptly declined as a result of the anti-Masonic movement in the United States which undermined Freemasonry's popularity. With the renewed popularity of Freemasonry in the second half of the 19th century, Masonic decoration returned to common use in a totally changed decorative style, characterized by a more Victorian and personal interpretation, and quite different from the earlier period.

Alan Gowans, author of *Images of American Living*, has stated that in the fifty years between 1775 and 1825, ". . . Masonic imagery seems to permeate American culture almost as Christian symbolism permeated the art of the Middle Ages."[2] How did the emblems of this 18th-century secret fraternal organization come to figure so prominently in the iconography of American art? Certainly, the widespread popularity of Freemasonry during this time and its patriotic associations with George Washington and other famous Freemasons of the Revolutionary period were factors. The explanation for the extensive use of Masonic symbols in American decorative arts is also found in the role that the symbolism and philosophy of Freemasonry came to play in establishing a distinctive American culture.

By the late 18th century, Freemasonry had gained wide acceptance in England, America, and the continent. An account book of a Philadelphia lodge, dated June 24, 1731, is the earliest extant record of an American lodge, although earlier accounts of British Masonic items in American newspapers suggest that Americans were familiar with Freemasonry before 1731.[3] From about 1730, Freemasonry in America grew rapidly and played an important role in the social and political history of the United States. Masonic lodges, like most 18th-century men's clubs, often met in public taverns and provided an important arena for the discussion and dissemination of ideas. For Americans removed from European centers of learning, Freemasonry provided a vehicle for the popularization and spread of new ideas which included the Enlightenment concepts of the equality of man, the power of reason over dogma, and the existence of natural laws. These radical ideas eventually formed the basis for American arguments favoring political separation from Great Britain.

Freemasonry also served as a unifying influence during the Revolutionary period. Relations among the American colonies in the colonial period had often been characterized by jealousies, territorial disputes, difficulties in communication, and widely diverse ethnic, social, and religious groups. By 1775, Masonic lodges had been established in each of the thirteen colonies, and Masonic affiliations served as a common denominator to help bring the divergent groups within the colonies into a national entity: "It created in a limited but very prominent class of people a feeling of American unity without which American liberty could not have developed—without which there would have been no United States."[4] At least nine of the signers of the Declaration of Independence and many of the military leaders of the Revolution were Freemasons. It has been claimed that eleven other signers of the Declaration had Masonic affiliation but their membership has not been authenticated.[5] George Washington's Masonic affiliation was thus an important part of his role as the country's military and political leader. Washington's encouragement of military lodges in the Continental army was an additional factor in holding the loyalty of his soldiers. In fact, Masonic ties and patriotism were so closely entwined during this period that they virtually merge in popular usage.

For America, as an independent nation seeking a unified cultural identity separate from Britain, Freemasonry provided an immediate set of images and a developed aesthetic philosophy upon which it could draw. American colonists had always looked to England as the arbiter of taste and fashion. Freemasonry itself had been transplanted to the colonies from England, just as styles of furniture and dress were imported. But just as American cabinetmakers had given their own interpretation to Chippendale furniture designs, Freemasonry in America had taken on its own special character. Without a nobility, membership was drawn from laborers and artisans, as well as wealthy merchants. The ideas of equality, reason, and the brotherhood of man, inherent in Freemasonry, had been translated into American independence and democracy. In searching for a style that would represent the newly formed United States, American craftsmen, many of whom were members of the fraternity, quite naturally turned to the well-known system of symbols that Freemasonry provided.

MASONIC SYMBOLISM

By the end of the 18th century, Freemasonry had established a set of symbols that were central to its organization and teachings, and well known to growing numbers of Freemasons in America. The moral tenets of Freemasonry, which the symbols represented, had encouraged the bid for American independence and they continued to influence the establishment of a government based on principles of equality, natural rights, and democracy. These symbols of Freemasonry were derived from common objects, religion, and the intellectual environment of 17th and 18th-century Europe in which Freemasonry developed. Introduced to Americans through Masonic regalia, engravings, and books, they developed stylistically into standard designs that were adopted as American decorative motifs and used on everyday objects as well as Masonic regalia.

The ritual importance of the symbols of Freemasonry, apart from their decorative use, should be emphasized. The fraternity is often described as "a matchless and almost perfect system of morality taught by symbols."[6] The use of common objects taken from experiences of everyday life as symbols of philosophical and moral ideas was an important aid to the educational aims of Freemasonry. Masonic lectures for the various degrees were accompanied by a tracing board which illustrated the visual symbols and served as a guide to the ideas being taught. George Oliver, a popular 19th-century British author, explained the role of symbols in Freemasonry: "every character, figure, or symbol delineated on the Tracing Boards or placed visibly before the eye in the Lodge possesses a moral reference and inculcates the practice of moral and social virtue."[7]

As Freemasonry evolved from craft guilds to a philosophical society, the tools of the stonemasons remained the primary symbols used to teach the moral and social philosophy of the organization. The trowel, for example, is described as:

> an instrument made use of by operative masons, to spread the cement which unites a building into one common mass; but we, as free and accepted masons, are taught to make use of it for the more noble and glorious purpose of spreading the cement of BROTHERLY LOVE. . .[8]

Other stonemasons' tools used in the symbolism of Freemasonry also represent attributes like Brotherly Love that were probably influenced by the 18th-century Enlightenment; the square is the emblem of virtue, the level symbolizes equality, and the plumb rule, uprightness.

Early Freemasonry was steeped in the ideas of the Enlightenment, a period of great intellectual activity in the cause of general education as a means to freedom from prejudice and social injustice. The unifying characteristic of Enlightenment thought was a faith in the power of Reason, and its ideal was the natural man, unfettered by dogma, following the universal principles that would unify all mankind. The stonemasons' guilds, preserving as they did the simple practical wisdom of ancient artisans, fulfilled this ideal and provided a basis for the development of Freemasonry's moral system. The Enlightenment qualities of Truth, Beauty, Nature, and Reason, expressed in architectural and mathematical principles, were aptly represented by the enduring examples of stonemasonry that included the Egyptian pyramids, Greek temples, and Gothic cathedrals.

William Preston, a prominent English Masonic author of the 18th century, was particularly influenced by Enlightenment philosophy. His *Illustrations of Freemasonry*, published in 1772, was one of the first printed explanations of the lectures and symbols and reflects his interest in education and its role in human betterment. Preston's *Illustrations of Freemasonry* formed the basis for most later versions of the lectures. Jeremy Cross, the celebrated American Masonic lecturer and ritualist, published his *True Masonic Chart* in 1819, basing it on Thomas Smith Webb's *Freemason's Monitor* which in turn was drawn from William Preston's *Illustrations of Freemasonry*. Continuing Preston's influence in his *Masonic Chart*, Cross explained the significance of the mallet and chisel to the Mark Master's Degree in terms that would have been familiar to Voltaire, Rousseau, and other 18th-century philosophers:

The Chisel morally demonstrates the advantages of discipline and education. The mind, like the diamond in its original state, is rude and unpolished; but as the effect of the chisel on the external coat soon presents to view the latent beauties of the diamond; so education discovers the latent virtues of the mind and draws them forth to range the large field of matter and space, to display the summit of human knowledge, our duty to God and man. . . What the mallet is to the workman, enlightened reason is to the passions: it curbs ambition, it depresses envy, it moderates anger, and it encourages good dispositions. . .[9]

Architecture was another important source for the symbols of Freemasonry. The pillars, columns, and arches of Masonic symbolism reflect the 17th and 18th-century interest in neoclassical architecture that is so central to the imagery and philosophy of Freemasonry. The two prominent architects of the 17th century, Inigo Jones and Sir Christopher Wren, were reputedly members of Masonic lodges. Inigo Jones was responsible for introducing England to Italian Renaissance architecture and the designs of Antonio Palladio that were based on ancient Roman architectural orders and rules of proportion. Wren followed as the style's great popularizer, virtually rebuilding London in the new classical style following the great fire of 1666. The classical orders of architecture, Ionic, Doric, and Corinthian are the symbols for the Masonic attributes of Wisdom, Strength, and Beauty.

Much of the architectural symbolism of Freemasonry is also concerned with the building of King Solomon's temple. The pillars topped with globes represent the entrance to the temple and the black and white mosaic floor representing the floor of Solomon's temple, is symbolic in Masonry of the good and evil in life.

The development of the symbols and philosophy of Freemasonry was also influenced by the 17th-century discoveries of Sir Isaac Newton and his laws of physics which marked a new era in scientific research, and sparked a great popular interest in the sciences and learning. It became fashionable for upper class gentlemen to dabble in the study of philosophy, architecture, and especially the mathematical sciences. Drawing-room experiments became a form of amusement as well as instruction. John Theophilus Desaguliers, a French Huguenot living in England, was a prominent Freemason and one of the leading 18th-century popularizers of Newtonian physics. His demonstrations of scientific experiments were especially popular with the nobility, and his resulting friendships with influential noblemen helped to attract their support and membership for the new organization of Freemasonry in which he was active.

The importance of science, and especially geometry and its initial letter "G" in the symbolism of Freemasonry, dates from the mid-18th century and reflects this fascination with science. By the 18th century, the widespread interest in science had resulted in the popularization of scientific and mathematical terminology into everyday speech so that even common metaphors were drawn from the sciences.[10] The French philosophers, Pascal and Fontanelle, both speak of the "geometric spirit." "A work on ethics, politics, criticism," Fontanelle tells us, ". . . is merely so much more beautiful and perfect if it is written in the geometric spirit."[11]

Additional symbols were added from other sources in the 17th and 18th centuries when literacy was the exception and symbols played an important role in everyday communication. Some of the symbols of Freemasonry are universal in western culture: the beehive of industry, the evergreen representing immortality, and the anchor of hope. Everyone was familiar with the religious symbolism of the cross, the ark, and the dove. The symbolism of death and immortality was particularly important in the 17th and 18th centuries when a widespread preoccupation with death was manifested in elaborate funerals, mourning jewelry, and graphically carved gravestones depicting the grim reaper and death's head. The skull and crossbones, the hour-glass, scythe, and coffin were commonly known symbols for death which were integrated into the Masonic symbolism.

Heraldry served as another source for the use of symbols. The five-pointed star of Freemasonry may have developed from the Knight's spur or molet of Christian Chivalry. The compasses, one of the most important symbols of Freemasonry, appeared on the arms of the Mason's Company of London of 1472, and also appeared on the arms of other building-trade guilds.

Masonic symbols were often used in typically armorial arrangements through the 18th and 19th centuries as designs on ceramics, Masonic jewels, and other American decorative arts. An early and unusual example is a Masonic purse, dated 1767, worked in wool and silk on linen. The interior has knitted pockets, which according to family tradition, were used to hold Masonic regalia. The owner, Persifor Frazer of Pennsylvania, was a Major in the American Revolution and commanded a brigade at the

POCKETBOOK, 1767
Photo Courtesy National Society of the Colonial Dames of America in the State of Connecticut.

Battle of Monmouth. The armorial aspects of the design are significant: the square and compasses, shaped like chevrons, frame an escutcheon and motto, both standard elements in heraldry. Another interesting example of Masonic heraldry is a watercolor painting, "The FreeMason's Arms," attributed to John Coles, Sr. Both Coles and his son, John Coles, Jr., were portrait and heraldic painters of coats of arms in Boston from 1796 to 1825. Masonic coats of arms were also used as designs on English ceramics imported to America. A creamware pitcher, (Cat. No. 107) dated 1820-30 includes an armorial design, Masonic symbols, and the inscription, "The FreeMason's Arms."

Early Masonic symbols exhibit considerable diversity and are sometimes difficult to decipher. This lack of uniformity was characteristic of 18th-century American Masonic symbolism and continued into the early 19th century. An unusual painting of Masonic symbols, probably used as a tracing board and with a history of being removed from a lodge in Devon, Connecticut in 1835, provides an illustration of an early variation (Cat. No. 15). Although some of the symbols in the painting are familiar, the arrangement is quite different from the standard designs as they are now known. The ark and dove, for example, are given a place of greater prominence than the square and compasses which enclose the letter "A", for architect, rather than the letter "G" for geometry. Some of the other initial letters which signify Celestial Architect, Science, Geometry, Nature, Reason, and Brotherly Love are not ordinarily part of Masonic symbolism.

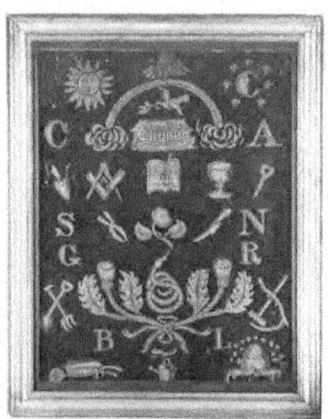

"MASONIC SYMBOLS," oil on canvas
Cat. No. 15.

Also included are the cup, a predominantly French symbol, and agricultural implements which are not part of any standard Masonic symbolism. The absence of standardized design and the use of obsolete initial letters and symbols would strongly suggest an 18th-century date for this painting.

The evolution of more standard Masonic symbolism is paralleled by the development of designs on Masonic aprons. The Masonic apron is itself a symbol, "the badge of a Mason," which is worn as part of the Masonic regalia. Based on the leather apron of 18th-century artisans, the earliest aprons were made of white lambskin symbolizing innocence and purity. Eventually the aprons were made of white silk shaped like a skin, and finally evolved into a square of silk edged with ribbon.

The practice of decorating aprons began in the last third of the 18th century. From about 1790 to the 1820's, aprons were handpainted, or embroidered with unique designs. The needlework aprons were probably made at home by women for family members. Painted aprons were almost certainly done by professional artists. From 1797 on, Ezra Ames, the famous Albany artist and a prominent Mason, describes painting Masonic aprons in his account books. Other artists in the early 19th century also did Masonic painting. John Samuel Blunt, a landscape and portrait painter of Portsmouth, New Hampshire, lists the painting of several Masonic aprons in his ledger of 1826 for which he charged between $1.75 and $2.25.[12] About 1810, aprons printed by professional engravers became popular and encouraged the growing trend toward more uniform designs. Engraved aprons were done by such well-known engravers as Amos Doolittle and Thomas Kensett, both of New Haven, Connecticut.

The art of the engraver came to play an important role in the development of more standardized Masonic symbols both in Europe and America. Engraving on wood or metal plates was important in the 18th and early 19th centuries as the only method of illustrating books, or publishing popular prints of historical subjects, town views, and portraits. By providing relatively inexpensive multiple copies, engravings also helped promote the dissemination of information and the development of styles. American artists, for example, used English engravings extensively as models for their portraits, and the prototypes of many American paintings can be traced directly to English mezzotints and engravings. With the expanded use of engraving to include printed decoration on textiles and ceramics in the late 18th century, the influence of English engraved designs in Ameri-

HANDKERCHIEF, printed by Gray & Todd, Philadelphia c. 1817. Collection of the Supreme Council, Ancient and Accepted Scottish Rite of Freemasonry, Southern Jurisdiction.

FRONTISPIECE, James Hardie, *New Freemason's Monitor*, N.Y., 1818. John Scoles, engraver.

ca was further increased. English Masonic engravings, which included book illustrations, sheet engravings, and decoration on objects, probably served as the main design sources for Masonic symbols used in America.

Cotton and silk handkerchiefs printed with copperplate engravings that included patriotic and historical subjects were popular from about 1750 to 1830, and undoubtedly played a part in establishing the designs for Masonic symbols. Masonic handkerchiefs were also printed during this period and may have been used as "tracing boards" for Masonic lectures. Many that were printed in England and imported to America definitely served as design sources. An interesting example is an engraved design for an apron and handkerchief that was printed in England in the 1790's. Consisting of the arch, pillars, "G" and the figure of a king, surrounded by various symbols, the design appears in several different versions on cotton handkerchiefs printed in America between 1810 and 1820. One example, "Engraved by Gray and Todd" was made by a Phila-

25

delphia firm working c. 1817. Some version of this handkerchief must have been familiar to the American engraver, John Scoles, who used the design for the frontispiece of James Hardie's version of the Masonic lectures, *The New Freemason's Monitor*, published in New York in 1818. The same design occurs again in a trompe l'oeil plaster painting found in Fuller Tavern, Berlin, Connecticut as part of the painted Masonic wall decoration in a room believed to have been used by the Berlin Masonic lodge. Done some time after the lodge was chartered in 1791, the Masonic symbols, the molded frame, and even a nail, are all painted directly onto the plaster to simulate a three-dimensional framed painting.[13]

English ceramics imported to America following American Independence were another source for designs. Transfer printing, developed in England in the 18th century, made possible the transfer of engraved designs onto ceramics. Many of the transfer printed Liverpool pitchers imported to America had Masonic decorations and inscriptions as well as patriotic designs. It is interesting to note that although the collections of the Grand Lodge in London include a wide variety of Masonic patterns on Liverpool wares, two Masonic patterns occur almost exclusively on pitchers made for the American market. This may be the result of the potters' practice of using stock patterns for Americans, but it also reflects the development of a distinctive American taste and style of Masonic decoration. Many of the symbols used in England were almost never used by American craftsmen, although Americans were familiar with them from the decorations on imported glassware and ceramics.

Masonic jewels are important examples of the work of American silversmiths and also contributed to the development of Masonic symbols. The first mention of uniform regalia appears in the records of the Grand Lodge of England's Quarterly Communication of June 24, 1727, when it was resolved that ". . . in all private Lodges and Quarterly Communications and Generall Meetings the Masters and Wardens do wear the Jewells of Masonry hanging to a White Ribbon. . ."[14] Eventually each office of the lodge had its own symbol, worn as a silver jewel of office. These included the Master's square, the Senior Warden's level, the Junior Warden's plumb, the crossed keys of the Treasurer, the crossed pens of the Secretary, the Stewards' cornucopias, the Tyler's crossed swords, the Chaplain's Bible and the Marshal's crossed batons. These jewels were made in sets for lodges and were owned and kept as the property of the lodge. During his term as Grand Master of Massachusetts from 1794 to

1797, Paul Revere[15] made several sets of officer's jewels for newly chartered lodges. One set, made for Washington Lodge, Roxbury, Massachusetts, at the time of its charter in 1796, is still owned by the Lodge, and is accompanied by the original bill of sale for £12. Another jewel associated with an office is the Past Master's Jewel, consisting of a quadrant and compasses, presented to the Master of a lodge at the end of his term of office. Although these were given to individuals, they were often returned and kept by the lodges. Many are quite elaborate and some included a diamond or other precious gem.

Several types of personal jewels were especially influential in establishing designs for symbols. During the period from 1780 to 1820, it was customary for Masons to have personal jewels made, often commemorating the date of initiation. There were no standard designs for these personal jewels. Silversmiths of the 18th and 19th centuries were commissioned to make jewels, and engraved them according to the individual's request. Jewels, however, were an easily transported item which could readily be copied by another craftsman. The fact that certain arrangements of symbols seem to recur on English and American jewels suggests that a certain amount of unofficial standardization was beginning. An interesting example of the repetition of designs is the caricature, "A Free Mason Form'd out of the Materials of his Lodge" by Samuel King of Newport, R.I., dated 1763. An almost identical design appears on an engraved jewel in the collections of the Grand Lodge of England entitled, "A Mason in full Dress, Lodge No. 133."[16] It is interesting to speculate whether the caricature was based on a version of this engraved jewel or whether both jewels might have used a common prototype such as a printed engraving.

An important factor in American symbolism is that it developed in the 18th century during a period of dispute in England over the number of degrees which should be included in the organization of Freemasonry. Following the practices of the trade guilds, members of Freemasons' lodges were first initiated into the degrees of Entered Apprentice, Fellow Craft, and Master Mason. One faction of Freemasons in England, "The Moderns," maintained that Freemasonry consisted only of these first three degrees. The other faction, "The Antients," adopted the further degrees of the Mark Lodge and Royal Arch Masonry, which they claimed were based on ancient Masonic traditions. This dispute finally culminated in a schism in the Grand Lodge of London in 1750, resulting in two Grand

Lodges, each claiming legitimacy. The split continued until 1813 when the two groups finally united under the United Grand Lodge and accepted Royal Arch Masonry as an integral, but separate part of, the Masonic system. During the years from 1750 to 1813, two rival Grand Lodges and the disputed degrees resulted in an expanded number of symbols and insignia which created a particularly rich period of symbolism and often provide clues to dating objects.

A great deal of the symbolism on American objects was influenced by the new degrees, since many of the American lodges were allied with the "Antients" in England. Of the ten military lodges in the Revolutionary army, for example, eight were "Antient."[17] Of particular interest are the Mark medals or jewels made by American silversmiths and engravers from about 1790 to 1830. As part of the Mark degree each member took a distinctive design as his own individual mark, following the practice of ancient stonemasons who supposedly used an identifying mark on their work. Most of the Mark jewels are round or shield shaped and are inscribed, "HTWSSTKS." The Royal Arch mottoes, "Holiness to the Lord" and "Virtue Shall cement us" are often included. Mark jewels were sometimes made in gold, as well as silver, and they often exhibit a particularly high degree of workmanship and originality of design. The Albany artist, Ezra Ames, recorded engraving Masonic jewels in his Account Book and also lists Albany silversmiths such as Isaac Hutton as patrons.[18] The fine quality of engraving on a particularly handsome Mark Jewel at the Albany Institute of History and Art suggests that possibly Ames, but certainly a professional artist, was responsible for the engraved decoration (Cat. No. 19).

Although the Masonic designs that appear on aprons, jewels, and ceramics indicate the beginning of more standardized symbols, a uniform American system of symbolism was first established in published form by Jeremy Cross in his *Masonic Chart*, published in 1819. Earlier publications of the ritual like Preston's *Illustrations of Freemasonry* and Thomas Smith Webb's *Freemason's Monitor*, had explained the meanings of the symbols but provided no description or illustration of their designs. Webb did not approve of the use of emblems to illustrate Masonic works, reflecting the greater secretiveness of the early fraternity. Cross made an important contribution to Masonic symbolism by including actual illustrations of the symbols which he hoped would correct inaccuracies in the ritual which he had observed in many American lodges during his tours as a

Masonic lecturer:

> Among these errors, may be mentioned, —the improper classification of masonic emblems; and a difference in the mode of working. To obviate these inaccuracies is the object of this work. It contains a classification of the emblems, together with illustrations, that have been approved and adopted by a majority of the Lodges of the United States.[19]

The engravings for the book were done by Amos Doolittle of New Haven, Connecticut, the well known engraver of the Battles of Lexington and Concord, and a member of the fraternity. Cross's book became immediately popular, and the Doolittle engravings quickly became the standard designs for American Masonic symbolism. Symbols, like the cock, that were found in 18th-century American symbolism, but not included in Cross's *Masonic Chart*, quickly fell out of use in America, although they continued in English Masonic symbolism. With the exception of the symbol of the Broken Column, which Cross and Doolittle are supposed to have originated, the symbols were based on the designs found on the ceramics, handkerchiefs, and jewels of the period. Cross and Doolittle took the informal but familiar Masonic designs found on objects used in America and published them in a standard source for future use and dissemination.

1775-1830

In attempting to establish a more distinctively American style, American craftsmen turned to the aesthetic philosophy and symbols of Freemasonry for their models. The "Federal style," which developed in the years following the Revolution, was based on European interpretations of classical designs, but was given an American identity by the use of patriotic symbols as decorative motifs. Freemasonry's reverence for classical forms of architecture as embodiments of the moral principles of the fraternity was firmly rooted in 18th-century thought which valued art for its literary and symbolic significance. Although more esoteric parallels with the ancient democracies of Greece and Rome may also have influenced the adoption of a classical style in America, the moral significance of classical forms in Masonic imagery was familiar to large numbers of Americans and made the classical revival in architecture and furniture especially appropriate as a national style expressive of the ideals of the new nation.

An extremely close relationship also exists between the development of patriotic symbols and the use of Masonic symbols in American decorative arts. The familiarity of American craftsmen with the symbols of Freemasonry and their use in decoration made it natural for them to use national symbols in a similar way. In some cases, the Masonic symbols themselves were considered emblems of patriotism.

Included among the American craftsmen who were Freemasons are silversmiths Nathaniel Hurd and Paul Revere who did Masonic engraving and also made Masonic jewels. John Frederick Amelung, a glassmaker in America from 1785 to 1795, was a prominent Mason and two presentation pieces attributed to his New Bremen, Maryland, factory have Masonic decoration. At least two American craftsmen used a Masonic symbol as part of their mark. William Nott, a pewterer working in Middletown, Connecticut and Fayetteville, North Carolina between 1813 and 1840, marked his pewter with an American eagle and the Masonic square and compasses above his name. Constantine Hope, a silversmith working in Savannah, Georgia from 1807 to 1809, marked his silver with his name, "HOPE," and the pseudo hallmark of a Masonic square and compasses in a serrated circle.

STOVE PLATE, H. W. Stiegel, Elizabeth Furnace, 1769. Photo courtesy Bucks County Historical Society.

Cat. No. 108.

One of the earliest examples of Masonic decoration associated with a prominent American craftsman is a stoveplate inscribed with the maker's name, "H. W. Stiegel Elizabeth Furnace 1769." Stiegel was the prosperous manager of the furnace and the founder of the only colonial glassworks in America. The classical Roman bust in the center of the plate is crowned with laurel and enclosed in a laurel wreath. To the left are the Masonic compasses and rule, symbolic of circumscribing the passions and dividing time between God, vocations, and rest. To the right of the bust are the square and level, representing virtue and equality. Made at the height of Stiegel's prosperity and success, it has been suggested that the bust represents Stiegel himself, "as a conqueror of difficulties."[20] If so, the Masonic symbols must represent the moral virtues that guided him. The stoveplate is thus an important instance of Masonic decoration which combines a classical design with Masonic symbols used to convey a moral message apart from the ritual significance of the lodge.

Following the pattern set by Freemasonry, American artists and craftsmen were able to develop a didactic art style using patriotic symbols to teach the principles and virtues of the new American society, much as Freemasonry taught its moral system. A striking example of the close relationship between patriotic and Masonic symbols appears on a Staffordshire plate of the States design made by James and Ralph Clews dating about 1830. The figure of America, holding a portrait of George Washington, wears the blindfold of justice and a Masonic apron, clearly linking Freemasonry with American patriotic symbolism. During this period of widespread use of Masonic symbols, which dates from 1775 and reached its peak from 1790 to about 1830, Masonic symbols appeared on almost every type of decorated object, whether alone, or in combination with patriotic symbols like the American eagle, Liberty, and George Washington.

One of the earliest examples of furniture with Masonic symbols specifically for use in a home rather than a lodge is a set of Chippendale style chairs made in 1788 as a wedding present for Captain Joseph McLellan, Jr., a ship captain of Portland, Maine. The Masonic square and compasses are worked into the design as a carved crest. More typically, furniture with Masonic symbols is found on Sheraton and Hepplewhite style furniture. The clean, straight, classically inspired lines of the Federal period were particularly suited to inlaid decoration of Masonic or patriotic symbols. Some fine examples of Masonic Federal style furniture include a late 18th-century secretary made in Massachusetts and inlaid with the square

TILT TOP TABLE
Courtesy Henry Francis
du Pont Winterthur Museum

and compasses, and a sideboard from New Haven, Connecticut in the Mattatuck Museum Collection with the Masonic pillars and globes as an inlaid design along each of the legs. A particularly interesting example of Masonic furniture is a Connecticut candlestand dated c. 1800, which combines the patriotic symbol of the eagle with the Masonic symbols of square and compasses, level and star.

Other furniture with Masonic decoration was specifically meant for lodge use. A decorated country chest, dating from the 1800-1820 period, was probably used in a lodge to store Masonic regalia (Cat. No. 82). The black designs of arches and pillars are stenciled over the typical red paint of the period. Several Masonic lodge rooms dating from the early 19th century, have been found with painted or stenciled wall decorations and it is interesting to speculate whether the chest might have been used in a room with similar stenciled decorations.

A 19th-century Master's chair made by John Luker for Worshipful Master J. H. M. Houston is another example of American painted furniture with Masonic decoration (Cat. No. 79). Houston was the master of Swan Lodge No. 358 in Vinton County, Ohio from 1867 to 1873. Chartered in 1866, the lodge dedicated a new building for its quarters in 1871, and it is quite possible that the chair was made at that time.

Utilitarian objects like stoneware jugs and crocks were also decorated with Masonic symbols. One example is a jar made by Justin Campbell of Utica, N.Y., in 1825. It was presumably presented to "P. Darrow of Rome" since his name is inscribed on the jar. It is decorated with a stylized Masonic apron, unusual in American symbolism, and the more typical plumb, setting maul, trowel, square, and compasses. The incised designs, filled with blue, are typical of this early period of stoneware. Later stoneware made after 1850 is also found with Masonic decoration, but it is usually the standard square, compasses, and "G" in blue slip decoration.

Two patterns of woven coverlets using Masonic symbols are attributed to 19th-century New York weavers. More complex coverlet patterns, requiring a Jacquard loom, were made by professional weavers who were often recent arrivals from Scotland and England. One coverlet pattern with the Masonic symbols of the pillars, square, and compasses combined with patriotic symbols of the eagle, liberty bell, and Independence Hall in the border design is attributed to James Alexander of Orange County, New York. One of the earliest examples of this coverlet, dated July 4, 1823, includes only the inscription: "Agriculture and Manufactures are

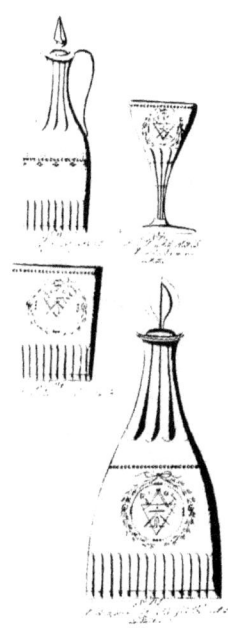

PATTERN BOOK
Courtesy Henry Francis
du Pont Winterthur Museum.

the Foundation of Our Independence." The next year, 1824, was the date of Lafayette's famous visit to the United States. Coverlets in this pattern dated 1824 and 1825 have the additional inscription: "GENRL LAFAYETTE," but later examples dated in the 1830's do not include Lafayette's name.

Another coverlet pattern of this period is also attributed to New York State although the weaver is not known. The pattern includes even more extensive use of the symbols. The border design combines almost all of the major Masonic symbols of the eye, star, pavement, anchor, and beehive, as well as the working tools of Masons. The trowel, and square and compasses are also worked into the medallions of the center design.

The development of American taste for Masonic symbols on decorative arts was also expressed in the choice of imported goods. Following independence from England, manufacturing was still undeveloped, and Americans remained dependent on European sources for most fine quality glasswares and ceramics until the mid-19th century. American preference for imported goods is strongly reflected in the advertisements of American craftsmen and dealers who constantly boast that their goods are equal to European manufactures. In 1825, for example, Thomas W. Dyott of the Kensington Glass Works advertised flasks, "and a variety of other Glassware, all of which is manufactured at the Philadelphia and Kensington Factories and in quality and in workmanship is considered equal and in many articles superior to English Manufacture."[21]

Like other fine glassware of the period, from the 1780's to the 1820's, most engraved Masonic glassware was imported from England, Germany, and Holland. A pattern book of German or Bohemian glass dating from c. 1800 originally belonged to the Gardiner family of Gardiner's Island, N. Y. The book includes a pattern of Masonic glassware that was available to Americans. (An example of this type of decanter is represented in No. 37 of the catalog.) Masonic glassware, including decanters, wine glasses, and tumblers, was used by wealthy families as well as by the Lodges, before restrictions on alcoholic beverages were instituted in America. A particularly Masonic form is the firing glass, with an especially heavy bottom, which was pounded on the table as a part of Masonic toasts.

Following American independence, British potters were eager to regain the lucrative American market. Even before the end of the Revolutionary War, Staffordshire potteries were prepared with black transfer printed designs on creamware that would appeal to the patriotic sentiments of Americans. Masonic patterns were among the popular designs that were combined with patriotic motifs for the American trade. Two common patriotic patterns were "Peace, Plenty, and Independence" with the United States Seal surmounted by an eagle (Cat No. 93), and the Seal surrounded by interlocking rings representing the states (Cat. No. 92). Both appear on pitchers with the most common Masonic pattern found on Liverpool pitchers for the American market. The design consists of two pillars and the mosaic pavement surrounded by floral and leaf sprays and surmounted by the allegorical figures of Faith, Hope, and Charity. Between the columns are Masonic symbols which include the sun, moon, and stars, the all-seeing eye, crossed pens, crossed keys, Euclid's Forty-seventh problem, pick and shovel, coffin, cock, beehive, and three candlesticks.

Another stock design on American Liverpool pitchers is signed by the engraver, James Kennedy, of Burslem, England. The pattern is similar except that the two pillars are labeled "J." and "B." and surmounted by the two wardens. A central column with the master's square, the mosaic pavement and a similar grouping of Masonic symbols are placed within the pillars. The whole is surrounded by sprays of flowers and leaves and topped by the symbol of Charity, represented by a mother and children.

A third Masonic design on Liverpool wares with a history of American ownership is found on a creamware mug with the impressed mark, "WEDGWOOD & CO.," of Ralph Wedgwood, an English manufacturer of stoneware and creamware from 1796 to 1800. The design is a version of the Freemasons' Arms with the inscriptions, "The Heart that Conceals and the Tongue that Never Reveals," and "Amor, Honor et Justitia," the motto of the "Moderns" in England before 1813. Several bowls with this same design have also been found in American collections.

Many of the Liverpool pitchers were meant as special presentation pieces to individuals or for lodges. One pitcher (Cat. No. 92) includes a sentimental engraving under the spout with the inscription "Friendship, Love and Unity, Accept this Pledge of Affection," suggesting that the pitcher was meant as a personal gift. A well documented presentation pitcher is the Boston Fusiliers pitcher (Cat. No. 89). One hundred of these pitchers were made by special order for Capt. Samuel Jenks in 1790, and presented to each member of his company. The uniformed fusilier is standing on the familiar Masonic black and white pavement. Above the oval framing him are the Masonic symbols of the all-seeing eye, sun, moon, and stars, the square and compasses, "G", and the level. Perhaps the symbol of the level was specifically used here to emphasize the equality of all members of the company. Samuel Jenks was a member of King Solomon's Lodge, Charlestown, Massachusetts, and the "Independent Fusiliers" led the procession at the Masonic celebration of laying the cornerstone of the New State House in Boston on July 4, 1795.

A pair of particularly handsome pitchers (Cat. No. 87) were especially made and presented to Union Lodge of Dorchester, Massachusetts, in 1811. The transfer decorations include the standard Masonic pattern with the figures of Faith, Hope and Charity, and an interesting engraving with the inscription "Veritas Praevalebit" (The Truth Will Prevail), probably illustrating an event in Masonic lore. The transfer under the spout is the insignia of the Grand Royal Arch Chapter of England before 1817, and the inscriptions "Cemented with Love" and "Holiness to the Lord" are both identified with Royal Arch Masonry. The name "Union Lodge" appears under the Royal Arch insignia. The minutes of the Lodge for June, 1811, leave little question about how these pitchers were used in early lodges; "the lodge voted its thanks to Brother Nehemiah W. Skillings, for his handsome present of two Masonic punch pitchers."[22]

Standard designs of ships also appear in combination with Masonic patterns on Liverpool wares, probably aimed to appeal to the ship captains involved in the English trade. Masonic inscriptions were also commonly used on pitchers with Masonic decoration. The Entered Apprentice's Song which begins "The World is in Pain, Our Secrets to gain. . ." was one of the most frequently used, and suggests that some of the pitchers may have been presentation pieces to newly initiated Masons.

Masonic symbols continued to be used in later Anglo-American china of the 1810-1830 period, which include hand-painted and printed earthenware and creamware. Luster decorated wares of this period also used Masonic transfer designs and inscriptions. One common type of Sunderland pitcher combines a stock Masonic design on one side with a view on the reverse of the Bridge over the River Ware, in England, that was dedicated with a Masonic ceremony.

Freed from British trade restrictions following American independence, Americans lost no time in establishing trade with China. The first American ship involved in the China Trade was the Empress of China, which sailed from New York in 1784. Other American merchants quickly followed and began importing teas, spices, silks, and ceramics. Chinese porcelain was a particularly important item. By the time Americans entered the China Trade, the Chinese had already developed certain stock patterns, several of which used Masonic symbols. Since symbolism plays an important part in Chinese art, Chinese decorators must have felt a degree of familiarity in working with designs of symbols. The most common stock pattern imported in the American trade is made up of polychrome symbols with either a star or grapevine border. The design includes an oval frame topped by a head of wheat enclosing the pillars and mosaic pavement. Among the symbols usually arranged around this oval are the beehive, a Chinese-type work bench and tools, the square, level, compasses, Bible, and a smooth ashlar fitted with a handle. Other versions include only the sun, moon, stars, and a cloudy canopy interpreted as stylized Chinese rain clouds. Another type of Masonic decoration imported to America were personal monograms with a pseudo-armorial design of Masonic emblems. The forms of Masonic decorated China Trade porcelain are primarily mugs, punch bowls, tea and coffee pots, and more rarely, entire tea sets. The notebook of an American trader dated 1797, in the collection of the Rhode Island Historical Society, lists the "Price current at Canton for Chinaware" and includes 1 to 1½ gallon Masonic bowls for 2 to 3 dollars each, and Masonic pint mugs for 20 dollars a hundred.[23] Most of this porcelain was probably for private use, although the history of some of the larger punch bowls definitely suggests that they were used in lodges.

Another oriental import with Masonic decoration was Japanese lacquer ware. Direct American trade with Japan dates from 1797-1801 when several American ships were chartered by the Dutch East India Company,[24] and then not again until after Commodore Perry's negotiations and the opening of Japan to American trade in 1854. Japanese goods, however, reached England and America through trade with the Dutch. Given the severe Japanese restrictions on contact with Westerners, the existence of Masonic designs on lacquer boxes raises the question of what design sources might have been used by the Japanese craftsmen. It is particularly interesting since one Masonic design is used almost exclusively on lacquer boxes from the late 18th to the mid-19th century (Cat. No. 114). The arrangement of symbols in a hexagonal frame is typical of the 18th-century English Masonic designs found on glassware and ceramics as well as regalia. It includes the familiar columns, globes, pavement, and tools as well as the more typically English symbols of a temple building and a tent. Many examples also include a bow topping the frame, suggesting that the design may have been taken from either a Masonic jewel suspended from a ribbon, or from an apron with silk ties.

One of the earliest documented pieces of this lacquer ware in America is a small Masonic decorated cigar box that has a history of having been presented to General Stevens by George Washington, thus dating it before 1799. Washington may have obtained the box as a gift from Houkgeest Van Braam, a Dutch merchant sympathetic to American Independence, or from another of his Dutch acquaintances.

In the period 1775 to 1830, Masonic symbolism was used on almost every type of decorated object used in America. Simple items like butter prints were often carved with a decorative motif, and some include Masonic symbols. Tavern signs were commonly painted with pictorial designs, and many display Masonic symbols, identifying the owner as a member of the fraternity, or the tavern as a Masonic meeting place. Gravestones carved with elaborate allegorical designs depicting death and resurrection were used throughout the 18th and 19th centuries, so it is not surprising to find carved gravestones with Masonic symbols. Similarly, engraved powder horns, often decorated with patriotic symbols, maps, and inscriptions, also used Masonic symbols as decoration.

Perhaps the most significant American products with Masonic symbols are the pictorial flasks that were produced by American glasshouses. From about 1810, bottles and flasks began to be blown into full size, two-piece molds which made the use of inscriptions and pictures possible as decoration. Masonic decorated flasks of this sort seem to be an exclusively American phenomenon. Fine engraved glass with Masonic symbols continued to be imported from England, Germany, and Holland. There is no evidence, however, that molded Masonic flasks like those made in America were ever made by European glass manufacturers. Masonic decorated flasks are also of special importance since they seem to have been among the earliest designs used on this type of flask:

> In fact, it may be said that from about 1810 or 1815 through the 1860's at least, decorative, pictorial and historical bottles and flasks were a national style of packaging some hard and some less ardent liquors. It is believed at present that some of the Masonic and decorative flasks preceded the historical.[25]

Over forty-six varieties of Masonic flasks were produced by the major American glasshouses between 1815 and 1830, corresponding with the fraternity's period of greatest popularity. The largest number of flasks were made by the Marlboro St. Works in Keene, New Hampshire. The different variations of the Keene flasks all include the Masonic pillars, arch, and pavement surrounded by different combinations of the other symbols. The reverse of the Keene flasks is an eagle and banner, often with the inscription "E Pluribus Unum." Several varieties of Pennsylvania and Ohio flasks in a more rounded shape combine the Masonic pillars, arch and pavement with the farmer's arms. A Zanesville, Ohio, flask (Cat. No. 50) shows an angry American eagle on the reverse, while a similar flask marked "Kensington Glass Works Philadelphia" has the frigate "Franklin" on the reverse and the inscription "Free Trade and Sailor's Rights" (Cat. No. 57).

Masonic symbols were also used on portrait flasks. The Marquis de Lafayette, both a hero of the American Revolution and a member of the Masonic fraternity, returned for a visit to the United States in 1824, sparking a great proliferation of objects commemorating the event. Examples of Lafayette flasks combined with Masonic symbols were made by Thomas Stebbins of Coventry, Connecticut, the Mount Vernon Glass Works, Vernon, New York, and Knox and McKee of Wheeling, West Virginia. One of the Thomas Stebbins flasks has a bust of Lafayette above the initials T.S. for Thomas Stebbins. The reverse is the Masonic arch, pillars, and pavement with triangle, square and compasses, sun and moon. The Mount Vernon flasks use a similar bust of Lafayette and the arrangement of Masonic symbols on the reverse is also the arch, pillars and pavement design, similar to the Keene flasks, and reflecting the importance of the arch in American Masonic symbolism of this period. The Knox and McKee flask places a bust of Lafayette within the Masonic arch and pillars and uses an American eagle as the decoration on the reverse.

About 1830, the production of Masonic flasks seems to end rather abruptly. This was probably a direct result of the anti-Masonic sentiment caused by the Morgan affair in 1826, and the growing influence of the temperance movement which made the use of Masonic symbols on whiskey flasks no longer acceptable. The immediate reaction of the American glass industry to these two changes in American society is strong evidence that the decorative arts of this period were, in fact, important and accurate expressions of the social and political feelings of the nation.

The use of Masonic symbols in America reached the height of its popularity in the decade between 1820 and 1830 and then ended rather abruptly. The end of this extremely rich period of Masonic symbolism was the result of growing anti-Masonic feelings in several quarters. The combination of Freemasonry's popularity and the political prominence of Masons like DeWitt Clinton and Andrew Jackson aroused severe criticism in political circles. Religious leaders resented the allegiance of its members to the moral system of Freemasonry and were suspicious of the deistic overtones of 18th-century Freemasonry's philosophy. A specific incident, the alleged kidnapping of William Morgan by Masons of Batavia, New York, in 1826, began a wave of anti-Masonic sentiment. Many lodges were forced to close and, with the popularity of Freemasonry severely undermined, Masonic symbolism as decoration virtually disappears.

THE VICTORIAN PERIOD

It took several decades for Freemasonry to regain some of its former popularity. During the Civil War, the formation of military lodges was probably an important factor in the renewed strength of the fraternity in the 1850's and 1860's. The revival of Freemasonry in the second half of the 19th century was accompanied by a new era of Masonic decoration. The post Civil War period was marked by many changes in American life, and decorative arts with Masonic symbols in the Victorian period reflect different values from those of the earlier period of the fraternity's popularity in America.

Alan Gowans has suggested that the teachings of Freemasonry continued to influence American culture as a factor in the development of Victorian aesthetics.[26] Freemasonry's interest in architecture and decoration as moral symbolism was certainly compatible with Victorian taste for historical revivals of Gothic, Renaissance, and Italian architecture. The earlier classical revival, so closely related to Freemasonry's symbols and teachings, was considered old-fashioned by the 1850's. A. J. Downing, whose books on landscape and architecture were carefully followed in the 1850's, sought to break away from the "Grecian style" and mourned the fact that, "nine-tenths of even the educated, believe that the whole circle of architecture is comprised in the five Orders; or at most that a Greek temple and a Gothic cathedral are the Alpha and Omega of the art."[27] It is possible that the "Grecian style" in architecture and furniture retained this tenacious popularity partly as a result of the emphasis on classical architecture in Masonic teaching.

The Victorian penchant for giving symbolic and literary interpretations to art may have been influenced by the teachings of Freemasonry.

Nineteenth-century Americans furnished their homes according to an aesthetic that was more concerned with the moral, social, or intellectual ideas implied in the styles of objects than for the beauty or utility of their forms. Downing himself preferred the new "Italian style," a combination of Italian and French architecture, because of its greater variety of ornament and the fact that "It addresses itself more to the feelings and senses and less to the reason or judgment than the Grecian style."[28] He also felt that it was "better suited to symbolize the variety of refined culture and accomplishment which belongs to modern civilization."[29]

If Victorian taste was indirectly influenced by the philosophy of Freemasonry, Masonic lodges and regalia were directly affected by Victorian styles. The Victorian historical revivals were particularly appropriate for the architecture of Masonic temples and lodge furniture. Abandoning the simplicity of the Federal and Greek Revival architecture of an earlier generation, Masonic lodges in the late 19th century eagerly sought the more eclectic use of historical styles currently in vogue. The Masonic Temple in Philadelphia, dedicated in 1873, is a perfect example of Victorian eclecticism. Designed by James H. Windrim, the exterior is based on Norman architecture. Each of the lodge rooms, Egyptian Hall, Corinthian Hall, Ionic Hall, Norman Hall, and Oriental Hall, is a sumptuous expression of a different architectural style representing various periods of stonemasonry. Although the effect is somewhat overwhelming today, to contemporaries whose homes were furnished in the "Gothic Style" or the "Modern French Style," it must have been the ultimate statement of historical revivalism.

Masonic regalia of the late 19th century was also influenced by contemporary Victorian taste for ornament. Masonic aprons ceased to be the delicately restrained painted and engraved aprons of the early 19th century and became ornate productions, heavily decorated with gold and silver bullion and embroidery. Masonic jewels were no longer handcrafted by silversmiths, but were produced by commercial jewelry firms. The designs for jewels became increasingly elaborate concoctions of the rococo scroll work and applied decoration that was popular on all types of Victorian silver.

Even the categories of objects that were decorated with Masonic symbols in the Victorian period differ from those of the earlier Federal period. Many of the different forms reflect the shift from individual craftsmanship to mass production and industrialization. Some of these objects with Masonic symbols are important because they are part of the new technology of the 19th century. For example, thermoplastic daguerreotype cases, made from a sawdust composition compressed under heat, were developed to provide more decorative cases for the new photographic likenesses. A molded thermoplastic case with Masonic decoration of pillars, arch and pavement, is labeled "S. Peck and Co.," and a similar design was used as a box lid made by the Scovill Manufacturing Co. of New York who also made daguerreotype cases.

The types of objects with Masonic decoration in the Victorian period also imply basic changes in American customs and attitudes which carried over into Freemasonry. In the second half of the 19th century, Masonic wineglasses and punch bowls were no longer standard items. Influenced by the Temperance Movement, Freemasonry had ceased to resemble an 18th-century men's club, and had carefully separated its ritual meeting from banquets and social functions. Still sensitive from the anti-Masonic period, the emphasis of Freemasonry's teachings moved further from 18th-century Enlightenment philosophy and deism and more closely paralleled established 19th-century religion.

Symbolism remained an important factor in Victorian decoration, but different symbols had come into vogue and were used in different ways. The Victorian love of flowers, for example, developed to the point that "the so-called 'language of flowers,' an elaborate and somewhat mystic code, played a role in Victorian friendship and courtship."[30] The patriotic and Masonic symbols, associated with Reason and the "rational man" of the 18th century, were replaced in the popular culture with more romantic and sentimental symbols. Although the symbols of Freemasonry remained the same, their usage more and more reflected the sentimentality of the Victorian period. The use of Masonic symbolism as decoration in the second half of the 19th century was no longer a national style, but rather a personal expression of involvement with Freemasonry on an individual level.

The personal use of objects with Masonic symbols is illustrated by the many 19th-century men's accessories that were commonly decorated with the symbolism. Shaving mugs and razors were often decorated with the square and compasses. Watch fobs were particularly suited to Masonic decoration, often identifying the wearer's membership in various branches of Freemasonry. The popularity of Masonic lapel pins, cuff links, and other men's jewelry dates from this period, and marks the beginnings of a new proliferation of commercial Masonic items.

Since the second half of the 19th century corresponds with the beginning of mass production, fewer items with Masonic symbols of this period are really of a quality to be considered as decorative arts. The most interesting examples are the pieces of individual handwork, many of which come under the category of "ladies fancy work" that was popular during this period.

Working with wax was considered an important art form among Victorian ladies who painstakingly fabricated realistic arrangements of blossoms and fruit, based on directions that appeared in the popular women's magazines of the period. The purity of white marble, simulated in wax, was considered especially appropriate for the wax crosses decorated with flowers which epitomize Victorian religious sentiment. An example of a wax Masonic square, compasses and "G", covered with tiny wax flowers expresses the same type of sentiment, and demonstrates the parallels between Masonic and religious symbolism of this period.

Perforated card embroidery, a new development in the second half of the 19th century, simplified embroidery by using a thin cardboard punched with holes. The card could be embroidered with wool and did not need to be blocked and stretched. By 1875, these cards were available with printed designs such as the many variations of the familiar "God Bless Our Home." At least two Masonic patterns were published, each with the inscription, "Trust in God," and a combination of the pillars, square and compasses, and Bible.

Late 19th-century quilting was another form of needlework which used Masonic symbols. Earlier pieced quilts did not lend themselves to the more complex Masonic symbols, although five-pointed stars are a common element of early quilt patterns. Applique quilts, popular after 1850, were much more suited to Masonic decoration. The technique of cutting small pieces of cloth into designs, turning under the edges and sewing them onto a background material with hemming stitches, made it possible to use the more complex Masonic symbols as designs. An extremely interesting quilt, dated around 1900, is one that was made as an album quilt by members of the Beacon Light Chapter, Order of Eastern Star, and presented to their sponsors, Beacon Light Lodge of Staten Island. Each of the thirty blocks, appliqued and embroidered with a Masonic symbol, was done by a different woman and then assembled. Another applique quilt of the late 19th century combines Masonic symbols with

QUILT DETAILS
Cotton applique, late 19th century.
Courtesy Mrs. Norman Lake.

more common designs of applique birds and "hit or miss" squares. Done in cotton, its design is similar to the silk and velvet crazy quilts of the 1870-90 period which also utilized Masonic and other symbols as decorative embroidery.

Most of the objects that were decorated with Masonic symbols during this period were either for the personal use of individual Masons or for use in lodges. Since many new lodges were chartered in the late 19th century and the old ones were renewed and expanded, many examples of lodge furnishings date from this period. One particularly interesting group is the woven carpeting with Masonic designs that was used in lodge rooms. Fragments of several different patterns dating from the 1850's to the 1880's have been located, and all those with a reliable history indicate that they were used as carpeting in lodges. Lamp globes with Masonic symbols of this period occur with some frequency and were probably also used in lodges. Lodge chairs were no longer individually made by craftsmen but could be ordered from furniture manufacturers. M. & H. Schrenkeisen of New York City included a section on "Church or Lodge Chairs" in their catalog for 1879. The several different variations illustrated are described as Gothic, Grecian, and Roman with the notation that "the above chairs can be made any desired height, also with Emblem of Lodges."[31]

CONCLUSION

The number of American objects with Masonic decoration is tangible evidence of the important role that Freemasonry has played in American life. The periods of Freemasonry's greatest popularity, in the years following American Independence and in the second half of the 19th century, are also the periods of the wide-spread use of Masonic symbolism. Even the decrease in the number of objects with Masonic decoration during the anti-Masonic period, is indicative of Freemasonry's political and social impact.

Masonic symbols used on American decorative arts reflect both the popularity of the fraternity and the current styles of the period in which they appear. Masonic symbols were displayed on the popular forms of the day. Punchbowls of the 18th century, and 19th-century lamps and lamp globes were decorated with Masonic symbols. Similarly Masonic decoration appears on Liverpool pitchers at the height of their popularity in the 1790 to 1810 period and on daguerreotype cases and crazy quilts of the late 19th century.

A strong case can also be made for the involvement of Masonic symbolism in the development of American iconography. Decoration on American objects shows that Masonic symbols were directly integrated into American design and used in conjunction with patriotic symbols in the late 18th and early 19th centuries. Less direct, but equally important, is the fact that familiarity with Freemasonry's use of symbols undoubtedly influenced the adoption of an American decorative style that utilized symbols to represent the ideals and aspirations of the newly formed United States.

During the period from 1775 to 1830, when Masonic symbolism and patriotic imagery virtually merged, Masonic decoration can truly be considered as a national style that went far beyond the exclusive use of the fraternity of Freemasonry. Following the decades of the anti-Masonic period of the 1830's to 1850's, Masonic symbols returned to popularity in a style that reflected a more religious, sentimental, and personal use of symbolism, and exemplifies the taste of the Victorian era in America.

After 1900, Masonic symbolism no longer plays a role in American decorative arts. Although Masonic symbolism continues to be used as decorative motifs by Freemasonry and its members, it is no longer a part of the popular American culture of the 20th century. Other symbols are used today as decoration, much as Masonic symbols were adopted in the 18th and 19th centuries. Perhaps the closest comparison in today's popular culture would be the great interest in astrology and the proliferation of the signs of the zodiac as decoration on sweatshirts, placemats, dishes, and other everyday items.

To the student of American culture, the phenomenon of Masonic symbolism as decoration represents an important chapter in the development of American taste and design. Regardless of whether Freemasonry shaped American taste or reflected current styles, its presence in American culture is significant. Masonic symbolism in American decorative arts remains an important field of research in the study of American art.

BARBARA FRANCO
Curator of Collections

FOOTNOTES

1. Several American lodge chairs of the 18th-century colonial period have been documented. One from the Boston area dated 1765-1785 (*Paul Revere's Boston*, Boston Museum of Fine Arts, New York Graphic Society, Boston: 1975, p. 213) and a Charleston Masonic chair dated c. 1770, (*Antiques*, January 1967), p. 109.

2. Gowans, Alan, "Freemasonry and the neoclassic style in America," *Antiques* (Feb. 1960), p. 172.

3. Tatsch, J. Hugo, *Freemasonry in the Thirteen Colonies* (New York, Macoy Publishing Co., 1929), p. 19.

4. Fay, Bernard, *Revolution and Freemasonry* (Boston, Little, Brown and Co., 1935), p. 230.

5. Case, James R., Foreword to *The Signers of the Declaration of Independence* (Bloomington, The Masonic Book Club, 1975).

6. Darrah, Delmar Duane, *History and Evolution of Freemasonry* (Chicago, The Charles T. Powner Co., 1951), p. 286.

7. Oliver, George, *Historical Landmarks of Freemasonry* (London, 1846), p. 74.

8. Cross, Jeremy, *Masonic Chart* (New Haven, 1819), p. 40.

9. *Ibid.*, p. 52.

10. Anderson, M.S., *Europe in the Eighteenth Century* (New York, Holt, Rinehart and Winston, Inc., 1961), p. 291.

11. Fontanelle, *On the Usefulness of Mathematics and Physics* (Paris, 1818).

12. John Samuel Blunt Ledger, 1821-1826, Collection of F. C. Tahk.

13. Little, Nina Fletcher, *American Decorative Wall Painting 1700-1850* (New York, Old Sturbridge Village and Studio Publications, 1952), p. 115.

14. *Grand Lodge 1717-1967*, United Grand Lodge of England (Oxford, University Press, 1967), p. 65.

15. Paul Revere II, 1735-1818, was the prominent Freemason who made the famous ride in 1775. His father, Paul Revere I was also a silversmith.

16. Hammond, William, *Masonic Emblems and Jewels, Treasures at Freemason's Hall, London* (London, George Philip and Son, 1917), plate 41.

17. Tatsch, J. Hugo, *Freemasonry in the Thirteen Colonies* (New York, Macoy Publishing Co., 1929), p. 210.

18. McClinton, Katherine Morrison, *Collecting American 19th Century Silver* (New York, Scribner's, 1967), p. 213.

19. Cross, Jeremy, *Masonic Chart* (New Haven, 1819), p. 6.

20. Mercer, Henry Chapman, *The Bible in Iron* (Doylestown, Pa., Bucks County Historical Society, 1961), p. 233.

21. McKearin, George and Helen, *American Glass* (New York, Crown Publishers, 1941), p. 457.

22. *An Historical Sketch of Union Lodge A.F.&A.M., Dorchester* (Boston, Spartan Press, 1926), p. 40.

23. Mudge, Jean McClure, *Chinese Export Porcelain* (University of Delaware Press, 1962).

24. The Dutch were the only Western nation allowed to trade with Japan at the time and then were allowed one ship a year.

25. McKearin, Helen, "Figured Bottles & Flasks," *Concise Encyclopedia of American Antiques*, Helen Comstock, ed. (New York, Hawthorn Books, 1969), p. 287.

26. Gowans, Alan, "Freemasonry and the neoclassic style in America," *Antiques* (February, 1960).

27. Downing, A. J., *The Architecture of Country Houses* (New York, D. Appleton & Co., 1854), p. 2.

28. *Ibid.*, p. 380.

29. *Ibid.*

30. Margaret Woodbury Strong Museum, *A Scene of Adornment* (Rochester, New York, 1975), p. 41.

31. Schrenkeisen, M. & H., *Illustrated Catalogue. . . of Parlor Furniture* (New York, 1879), p. 52-54.

GLOSSARY OF SYMBOLS

In a symbol there is concealment, and yet revelation here, therefore by Silence and by Speech acting together, comes a double significance And if both the Speech be itself high, and the Silence fit and noble, how expressive will their union be. Thus in many a painted Device, a simple Seal-emblem, the commonest Truth stands out to us proclaimed with quite new emphasis.

Thomas Carlyle
Sartor Resartus

EYE

ACACIA
Sprig of acacia a symbol of immortality.

ALL-SEEING EYE
A symbol of watchfulness and the Supreme Being, "whom the Sun, Moon, and Stars obey and under whose watchful eye even Comets perform and even invades the inmost reaches of the Human heart."

ANCHOR
Hope and a peaceful harbor for the weary.

APRON
The badge of a Mason. Usually white lambskin or white silk symbolizing innocence and purity. Originally a long leather apron similar to the type worn by 18th-century artisans.

ARCH
Symbol of the "arch of heaven" and Royal Arch Masonry.

ANCHOR

ARK
With an anchor, the symbol of hope and a well spent life. With a dove, the symbol of a degree known as the "Ark and Dove" formerly associated with Royal Arch Masonry.

ASHLAR
A hewn stone. The rough ashlar symbolizes man's imperfect state by nature. The perfect ashlar symbolizes the state of perfection arrived at by virtuous education.

B. Beauty
One of the principle supports of the Lodge together with Wisdom and Strength. Represented by a Corinthian column.

B. Boaz
"In strength." One of the two pillars of King Solomon's Temple.

ARK

BEEHIVE

CONSTITUTIONS

BROKEN COLUMN

BEEHIVE
Industry.

BIBLE
Symbol of the divine will of God. An open Bible often appears with a square and compasses, representing the Great Lights of the Lodge. An open Bible is also the jewel of the Chaplain.

BLAZING STAR
Divine providence, prudence.

BLUE
The color of symbolic Masonry representing the canopy of heaven. The first three degrees are known as the "Blue Lodge."

BOOK OF CONSTITUTIONS GUARDED BY THE TILER'S SWORD
Symbol of watchfulness and the unchangefulness of the Masonic Fraternity.

BROKEN COLUMN
Shown with a figure of Time and a weeping virgin standing over a book. Symbolic of mourning. The origin of this symbol has been attributed to Jeremy Cross's *Masonic Chart* published in 1819. The original engraving was done by Amos Doolittle.

CABLE-TOW
Symbolic of the scope of a man's reasonable ability. Associated with the Entered Apprentice degree.

CANDLES
Three candles represent the three Lesser Lights of the Lodge, symbolizing the sun, moon, and the Worshipful Master of the Lodge.

CARDINAL VIRTUES
Temperance, a figure measuring from a pitcher; Fortitude, a figure with a soldier's helmet; Prudence, a figure contemplating a mirror; Justice, a figure holding a scale.

CHARITY
The greatest of Masonic virtues. The third rung of the theological ladder. Often represented by a mother and children.

CHISEL
Combined with the mallet or maul, symbolic of the polishing effect of education and discipline on the human mind. The working tools of the Mark Master degree.

COFFIN

COLUMNS

CLOUDED CANOPY
The covering of a Lodge, symbolically the vault of heaven, demonstrating the universality of Freemasonry.

COCK
Symbolic of resurrection.

COFFIN
Symbolic of death.

COLUMNS
Two columns represent the two pillars of King Solomon's Temple. Three columns are the supports of the Lodge: Wisdom, Strength, and Beauty.

COMET
Used from 1735 to 1843, and then abandoned at the Baltimore Convention as being sectarian because of its resemblance to the Star of Bethlehem. (See All-seeing eye.)

COMPASSES
Symbolically used to circumscribe desires and keep passions in bounds.

CORNUCOPIA
Jewel of the Stewards of the Lodge.

CROWNS
Three crowns are associated with Royal Arch Masonry especially during the period of the Ancients in England from 1750-1813. Three crowns appear on the Seals of the Grand Lodge at York, England, between 1725 and 1779.

CUP
The cup of bitterness. Associated with the first degree of the French rite, it symbolizes misfortune and sorrow.

DOVE
Used as a symbol of a messenger in English Masonry. Appears only in the "Ark and Dove" degree in this country.

E. The East
Symbolic of light and knowledge.

EAR
The attentive ear symbolizes that we learn more from listening than from talking.

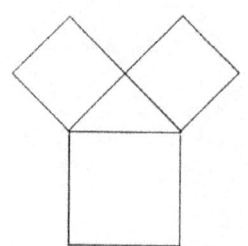
EUCLID

LADDER

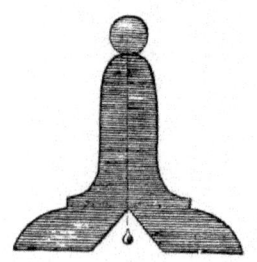
LEVEL

FAITH
The lowest rung of the theological ladder. Represented by a figure with a cross.

FORTY-SEVENTH PROBLEM OF EUCLID
Teaches Masons to be lovers of the arts and sciences.

G. Geometry or God
Introduced in the mid-18th century, it is usually shown suspended in the East. It is commonly used with the square and compasses as a decorative device, especially after c. 1850.

GAVEL
The hammer used to break off rough edges of stone symbolizes divesting the heart of vice.

GLOBES
Symbolic of the universality of Freemasonry. One celestial and one terrestrial globe appear on the pillars, J. and B.

HANDS
Symbolize giving and receiving signs of recognition. Clasped hands symbolize Fidelity.

HOPE
Second rung of the theological ladder. Represented by a figure with an anchor.

HOUR GLASS
Symbolic of human life.

J. Jachin, "God will establish."
One of the two pillars of King Solomon's Temple.

KEY
Symbolizes silence and secrecy. Crossed keys are the Treasurer's jewel.

LADDER
Jacob's ladder or the theological ladder of Faith, Hope, and Charity.

LAMB
Symbolic of innocence and purity.

LEVEL
Symbol of equality. The Senior Warden's jewel.

PLUMB

INCENSE

MAUL
Setting maul is a symbol of untimely death. Also see Chisel.

PAVEMENT
The Mosaic Pavement, Indented Tessel Border, and Blazing Star represent the floor of King Solomon's Temple. The black and white pattern is symbolic of the good and evil in life.

PENS
Crossed pens, Secretary's jewel.

PILLARS
Two pillars, J. and B. placed at the entrance of King Solomon's Temple.

PLUMB RULE
Symbolizes uprightness. Junior Warden's jewel.

POINT WITHIN A CIRCLE AND PARALLEL LINES
Introduced about 1730 as a symbol. The point represents an individual Mason and the circle the boundary line of his conduct. The parallel lines represent St. John the Baptist and St. John the Evangelist, patron saints of Masonry. Other explanations are also given for this symbol.

POT OF INCENSE
Emblem of a pure heart.

S. Strength
One of the three supports of the Lodge together with Wisdom and Beauty. Represented by a Doric column.

SCALES
Symbol of Justice.

SCYTHE
Emblem of time. Used more commonly in Ireland than in England.

SERPENT
A rod turned into a serpent is mentioned in the Royal Arch degree. A serpent swallowing its tail is a symbol of eternity or eternal life and is also used in Masonic symbolism.

SHOE
Associated with the first degree and symbolic of consecration and assumption of obligations.

SPADE
Symbolizes Divine Truth is discovered only through human efforts and death.

STAR

SWORD

SQUARE
Emblem of virtue. The Master's jewel.

SQUARE AND COMPASSES
Symbolize reason and faith. With a sun, the Senior Deacon's jewel. With a moon, the Junior Deacon's jewel.

STAR
Seven stars symbolize the number needed to make a perfect lodge. Five-pointed star symbolic of the five points of fellowship. Six-pointed star of double triangle called Solomon's Seal.

STEPS
Symbolize advancement in Masonic knowledge. Three steps symbolize the three stages of human life: youth, manhood, and age, as well as the first three degrees.

SWORD
The symbol of justice. Flaming (wavy) sword or crossed swords, the Tiler's jewel.

SWORD POINTING TO A NAKED HEART
Demonstrates that "justice will sooner or later overtake us."

TASSELS
The derivation of this symbol is not clear. H. W. Coil suggests that misunderstandings in translation resulted in the use of "tassels" on French and German tracing boards rather than the "tessel" border of the Mosaic pavement. Tassels appear on the frontispiece of an English edition of "Mah-ha-bone or the Grand Lodge Door Opened" as early as 1766. The cord and tassel may be a representation of the cable-tow.

TRIANGLE
Symbolic of deity.

TROWEL
The symbolic tool that spreads the cement that unites Masons in brotherly love. Used as the badge of the Grand Master in Ireland from c. 1725.

TWENTY-FOUR INCH GAUGE
Symbolizes the 24 hours of the day divided into three equal parts devoted to God, usual vocations, and rest.

W. Wisdom
One of the three principal supports of the lodge together with Strength and Beauty. Represented by the Ionic column.

CATALOG

Behold a Master Mason rare,
Whose mistic Portrait does declare,
The secrets of FreeMasonry
Fair for all to read and see;
But few there are to whom they're known,
Tho they so plainly here are shown.

Signed and dated under the inscription, "S. King pinx 1763".
Samuel King (1749-1819) was born in Newport, Rhode Island, and spent most of his life there as a nautical instrument maker and portrait and miniature painter. There is a tradition that he was sent to Boston to serve an apprenticeship as a house painter in the 1760's and may have studied other forms of painting as well. Marvin S. Sadik (*Colonial and Federal Portraits at Bowdoin College*, Bowdoin College Museum of Art, 1966, p 103) has suggested that he may have studied at the "atelier of Thomas Johnston where all manner of the decorative arts was practiced." Signed, "S. King 1763," this watercolor, done at the age of 14, would certainly reinforce the theory of a Boston apprenticeship. Now owned by St. Andrew's Lodge of Boston, it was probably done for a member of that lodge. The date 1758 at the base of the columns probably refers to the date of an individual's being raised a Master Mason. A similar design appears on a Masonic jewel in the collection of the Grand Lodge of England (William Hammond, *Masonic Emblems and Jewels,* Plate 41). It is probable that King used either a similar jewel with this design or a printed engraving as his model.

1

2
HANDKERCHIEF
England, c. 1810
Silk, 30" x 30"
Museum of Our National Heritage Collection
Gift of Earl W. Barton

Copperplate engraving printed in brown on white silk. The use of the "Antient" Grand Lodge of England arms dates this handkerchief design before 1813. The central design of arches, pavement, and symbols is surrounded by individual symbols framed in circles that are intertwined with wheat and leaves.

1
"A FREE MASON FORM'D OUT OF THE MATERIALS OF HIS LODGE"
Samuel King, 1763
Ink and watercolor on paper, 13 3/4" x 8 3/4"
Lent by St. Andrew's Lodge, A. F. & A. M., Boston, Massachusetts

The inscription below the figure is framed in a Rococo oval and reads:

3
HANDKERCHIEF
American, c. 1810-1820
Cotton, 20" x 22"
Lent by Chicago Historical Society

Copperplate engraving printed in red on cotton. A popular and often repeated design of pillars, arch and pavement with the figure of a king standing under the "G". The initials "W.M." are embroidered under the arch of the rainbow and may stand for an individual or "Worshipful Master."

4
HANDKERCHIEF
American, c. 1810-1820
Cotton, 20 7/8" x 24 1/2"
Lent by Old Sturbridge Village

Similar to No. 3 but with a Masonic Song below the main design which begins, "Arise and Blow thy Trumpet Fame, Freemasonry aloud proclaim." A similar handkerchief in the collection of the Supreme Council, Ancient and Accepted Scottish Rite of Freemasonry, Southern Jurisdiction, with the same song, was engraved by Gray and Todd working in Philadelphia in 1817.

5
TALL CLOCK
Luman Watson, Cincinnati, Ohio, c. 1816-1825
Cherry, 8'2" high x 18" wide
Lent by Mr. and Mrs. Charles V. Hagler

6
TALL CLOCK
Silas Hoadley, Plymouth, Connecticut, c. 1808-1825
Cherry, 7'3" high x 18 1/2" wide
Lent by the Essex Institute

Both the Hoadley and Watson clocks have a Masonic face with the same design of pillars, arch, and symbols. Although one was made in Connecticut and the other in Ohio, they are both in the Connecticut clockmaking tradition.

Luman Watson was born in Connecticut in 1790 and moved to Cincinnati about 1808 where he was associated with the clockmaking partnership of Read and Watson. It is not clear whether Luman himself was the partner at the age of 18, or whether he was working with his father, John Watson. In the spring of 1815, the partnership was apparently dissolved and Luman Watson returned to Connecticut. The records of Federal Lodge No. 17 of Watertown, Connecticut, show that Luman Watson was initiated and subsequently raised a Master Mason in June, 1815.

The account books of Ephraim Downs, a Connecticut clockmaker, provide further information about Luman Watson's activities in 1815. Downs' account books record work done for Read and Watson in April, 1815, and on October 8, 1815, record, "Luman Watson Dr. to 10 1/2 days work at the engine." (John A. Diehl, "Luman Watson Cincinnati Clockmaker," *Antiques*, June 1968, p. 796).

The association between Downs and Watson may have developed from a childhood friendship since they were close in age and grew up in neighboring towns. Downs apparently

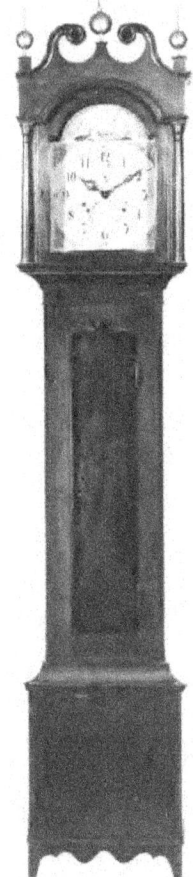

helped Luman Watson set up his clockmaking shop in Cincinnati in 1816. Between 1816 and 1821, he made two trips to Cincinnati with clock patterns and machinery, and the works of early clocks with Luman Watson's label are also marked "E.D." With Downs' help, Watson was able to advertise by 1829 that his clocks were "Warranted superior to any brought from the eastern states" (Ibid.).

The relationships among the various Connecticut clockmakers were close. Ephraim Downs and Silas Hoadley became brothers-in-law by marrying two sisters. In 1817, Hoadley joined the same Masonic Lodge, Federal No. 17, that Watson had joined two years earlier. Downs also joined the Masonic fraternity in 1817 as a member of Harmony Lodge in Waterbury, Connecticut.

Watson's return to Connecticut in 1815 and his close ties with other Connecticut clockmakers like Downs and Hoadley help explain the similar faces of these two clocks. Watson may have continued to import painted faces from Connecticut, or at least used a pattern brought from Connecticut.

7
TRUNCHEON
Massachusetts, c. 1796-1800
Carved wood, 22"
Museum of Our National Heritage Collection
Gift of Union Lodge A.F.&A.M., Dorchester, Massachusetts

Carved, gessoed and gilded wood, the center covered with blue velvet. The minute book of the Grand Lodge of England for 29 January, 1730, notes that the Marshal brought up the rear of a Masonic procession, "with his Truncheon Blew, tipt with gold" (Grand Lodge 1717-1967, p. 69). This similar blue and gold truncheon belonged to Union Lodge, A.F.&A.M., Dorchester, chartered in 1796.

8
TRUNCHEON
Massachusetts, c. 1796-1800
Carved wood, 19"
Museum of Our National Heritage Collection
Gift of Union Lodge, A.F.&A.M., Dorchester, Massachusetts

Carved, gessoed and painted wood, also blue and white with gilded ends. Originally belonged to Union Lodge, A.F.&A.M., Dorchester, chartered in 1796.

9
DOORKNOCKERS
Massachusetts, early 19th century
Brass, 5 1/2" x 3 1/2"
Lent by Russell Ward Nadeau

Doorknockers cast in a design of the Masonic pavement, broken column, square, compasses, level, plumb and 24" gauge. Doorknockers are placed on both sides of the doors to lodge rooms and are used to signal during the ceremonies. Another set of these doorknockers is still owned by the Simon Robinson Lodge, Lexington, Massachusetts.

10
SQUARE AND COMPASSES
Paul Revere, Boston, Massachusetts, 1796
Gilded brass, 6 3/4" diam.
Lent by Mr. Russell Ward Nadeau

Cast brass symbol of the square, compasses, "G", and cable-tow. A note attached to the casting stated that it was given to the Lodge by Grand Master Paul Revere for use on the closed altar Bible. It was probably cast by Revere at his brass foundry. The Lodge was probably Fayette Lodge, Charlton, which was chartered in 1796 during Paul Revere's term as Grand Master of Massachusetts.

10

11
DRAWER PULL
19th century
Brass, 4 1/2" x 5 1/2"
Lent by the Grand Lodge of Massachusetts, A.F. & A.M.

A pair of brass drawer pulls or handles with a design of square, compasses, and clasped hands. They were possibly used as handles on a Masonic altar.

12
DOORKNOCKER
19th century
Brass, 7 1/4" x 7"
Lent by the Grand Lodge of Massachusetts, A.F. & A.M.

12

A square, compasses and "G," and hand holding a gavel. Removed from a house at 10 Marshall St., Boston, before 1910.

13
OFFICERS' JEWELS
Charles Brewer, Middletown, Connecticut, c. 1812
Silver, c. 3 1/2"
Lent by St. John's Lodge No. 2, A.F. & A.M., Middletown, Connecticut

Set of 12 jewels made for St. John's Lodge.

14
OFFICERS' JEWELS
Paul Revere, Boston, Massachusetts, 1796
Silver
Lent by Washington Lodge, A.F. & A.M., Lexington, Massachusetts

Made by Paul Revere, Grand Master of Massachusetts, for Washington Lodge, Roxbury, at the time of its charter in 1796. The Lodge later moved to Lexington.

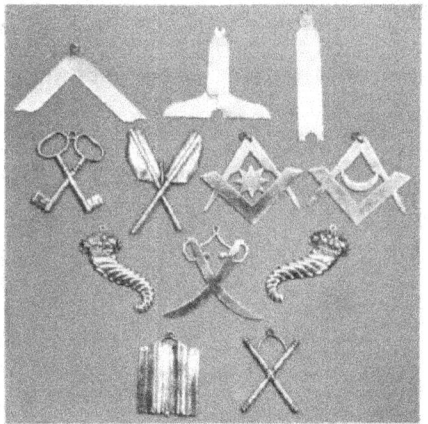

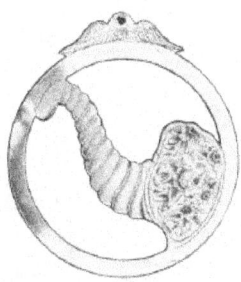

15
"MASONIC SYMBOLS"
Artist unknown, Connecticut, c. 1790-1810
Oil on Canvas, 21 1/2" x 16 1/2"
Lent by Mr. and Mrs. Gerald E. Knicely

The tradition associated with this painting is that it was removed from a Masonic Lodge at Devon, Connecticut, in 1835. There are no records of a lodge at Devon, but in all probability it was an early lodge which was forced to close during the anti-Masonic period of the 1830's and its records have been lost.

16
PIN
Providence, Rhode Island, c. 1813
Silver and paste, 1" x 7/8"
Museum of Our National Heritage Collection
Gift of Mrs. Fay C. Speers

A small pin with Masonic symbols mounted on blue metallic paper under glass. The back opens to show a tintype. It belonged to John T. Jackson who was admitted to Providence Royal Arch Chapter No. 1, June 17, 1813.

17
WATCH
Utica, New York, c. 1828
Silver, 2 1/4" diam.
Lent by Munson-Williams-Proctor Institute

Several of these English two case watches were engraved with Masonic symbols for Alfred Munson and other prominent Uticans by James Murdock, a Utica silversmith.

18
"FREEMASON'S ARMS"
John Coles, Sr., Boston, before 1809
Watercolor on paper
Lent by Old Sturbridge Village

Attributed to John Coles, Sr., a heraldic painter who worked in Boston between 1796 and 1809. His son, John Coles, Jr., was also a heraldic painter and worked in Boston from about 1809-1825. Bro. John Coles is mentioned in the Grand Lodge of Massachusetts Proceedings in 1796 and 1797.

19
MASONIC MARK JEWEL
Albany, New York, c. 1800
Gold, 3 5/8" x 2 1/2"
Lent by Albany Institute of History and Art

The obverse is engraved "James Skelding/Albany;" "HTWSSTKS" in a circle around the "mark" of a figure holding a scales. The reverse is engraved with seven circles each containing a Masonic illustration. A sun at the top of the jewel forms a crest and the crescent moon is placed at the bottom.

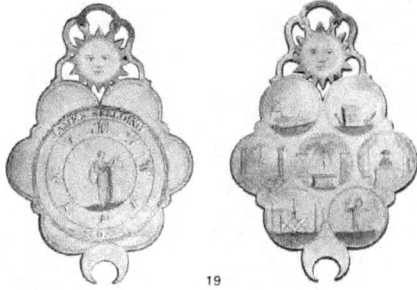

19

20
MASONIC MARK JEWEL
Albany, 1802
Silver, 3" x 1 7/8"
Lent by Albany Institute of History and Art

Obverse engraved, "Virtue shall cement us" and "HTWSSTKS" in a circle around an ark. Reverse engraved "Abraham Myers/5802." A winged cupid's head forms a crest, and the central design is a hand holding a rule with the working tools of Freemasonry balanced at either end.

21
MASONIC JEWEL
Albany, before 1813
Gold, 1 5/8" x 1 1/8"
Lent by Albany Institute of History and Art

Obverse engraved, "Sit Lux et Lux Fuit," above the pillars, arch and pavement surrounded by symbols. Reverse engraved with the initials "A.L.," the Freemason's arms and the motto "Amor Honor et Justitia" associated with the "Modern" Grand Lodge of England before 1813.

22
MASONIC MARK JEWEL
Connecticut, 1808
Silver, 3 3/8" x 2"
Lent by Grand Lodge of Massachusetts, A.F. & A.M.

Shield-shaped Mark medal. Obverse engraved with three concentric circles, a crest of the all-seeing eye and "Solomon Chaptr /Derby" at the bottom. Outer circle engraved with five Masonic symbols and "Chauncy M. Hatch." Second circle engraved "HTWSSTKS." Inner circle engraved with eagle holding anchor in its claws and Masonic square and compasses in its beak. Reverse engraved "Friendship & Union" with symbols of dove, serpent and cross, crown, and scales. "G" in a triangle in crest, "1808" engraved at the bottom.

23
MASONIC MARK JEWEL
Massachusetts, 1799
Silver, 3 3/4" x 2 1/4"
Lent by Grand Lodge of Massachusetts, A.F. & A.M.

Compasses, quadrant, and circle engraved, "The Property of Timothy Bigelow/Mark/Lodge/Boston/Massachusetts/1799." Outside of circle engraved "HTWSSTKS," center engraved with seven stars.

24
MASONIC JEWEL
c. 1800
Silver, 2" x 1 3/8"
Lent by Grand Lodge of Massachusetts, A.F. & A.M.

25
MASONIC JEWEL
Maryland, 1804
Silver, 2 1/2" x 1 5/8"
Lent by Mr. Donald Noble

25

24

Although little is specifically known about the history of these two jewels (24 and 25), their designs are remarkably similar. A third jewel with this same design, in the Museum of the Grand Lodge of Maryland, is inscribed "Hiram Lodge #28, 5801." This lodge met in Frederick, Maryland, until 1808. Since one jewel has a Maryland history and another is in a Massachusetts collection, it would appear that all three used a similar design source. They were definitely executed by different artists, judging from the quality of the engraving. The engraving of 24 is cruder than 25 and the design is somewhat simplified.

The main elements in both jewels are the arch, pillars, symbols and "W.S.B." for Wisdom, Strength, and Beauty on one side, and the ark, beehive, and other symbols on the reverse. Both include the initial letters "H.A." for Hiram Abif and "J.J.J." which refers to three of the characters associated with the Master Mason degree.

The Royal Arch references are even more specific in 25 and include "B.S.J.T.M.C." for Beauty, Strength, Justice, Temperance, Moderation, and Charity, and "G.R.L.A.G.M.A." which probably stands for Grand Royal Lodge Arch Grand Master Architect. "Joppa" refers to the ancient Biblical city of Joppa. "E" and "W" represent East and West. The initials "IL" and date 1804 could be the silversmith or engraver's mark, but they are more probably the initials of the owner.

The engraving and the added decorative element of the scalloped edge of 25 make it a particularly fine example of this type of engraved Masonic jewel.

26
MASONIC JEWEL
1803
Silver, 2 3/16" x 1 9/16"
Lent by Henry Ford Museum

Oval jewel engraved, "Bela Markham, Initiated April 13, 5803/Amor Honor Justitia."

27
MASONIC MARK JEWEL
Francis Shallus, Philadelphia, 1812
Gold, 2 3/16" diam.
Lent by Henry Ford Museum

Circle with keystone hung in center. Obverse engraved, "Mark Wilks Collet/Lodge 51 July 20th 1812" around circle. Keystone engraved with arch, pillars, pavement, three crowns, and "Shallus fecit." The reverse is engraved, "HT/ST/KS/WS" and with a scene showing the serpent and cross on the keystone. Francis Shallus was an engraver who worked in Philadelphia from 1797 to 1821.

27

28
MASONIC MARK JEWEL
Greensborough, North Carolina, 1830
Gold, 1 5/8" diam.
Lent by Henry Ford Museum

Circular shape engraved with pillars, arch, symbols, and inscribed, "R. Mitchell/1830/T.I. Sears F. Dusch." Reverse engraved, "Chorazin Chapter N 13/Greensborough N.C. Nov. 9, 1829." "HTWSSTKS" and square, compasses and crescent moon inside keystone.

29
MASONIC MARK JEWEL
c. 1800-1830
Silver, 3 1/2" x 2 3/8"
Lent by Henry Ford Museum

Heart shape, engraved with pillars, arch, pavement, and inscription, "John Tully/Orange MML N. 4." Reverse engraved with "HTWSSTKS" and plow. Orange is probably Orange, New Jersey, and the Masonic Mark Lodge was No. 4.

30
MASONIC JEWEL
1796
Silver, 2 9/16" x 1 9/16"
Lent by Henry Ford Museum

An oval jewel inscribed "Roger Ransteet Initiated May 11th 1796/Amor Honor et Justitia." This jewel represents another interesting connection when it is compared with 26. Again, both jewels have the same basic design. The motto of Amor Honor et Justitia is associated with the "Modern" Grand Lodge of England before 1813, and the absence of the arch in the design is in keeping with the "Modern" lodges. Obviously done by different engravers, the earlier medal is boldly drawn, while the later medal is less assured. Again we can conjecture whether the design of the later medal was copied from the earlier one, or whether both are copies of a similar prototype.

26

30

31
MASONIC APRON
Massachusetts, 1790's
Leather, 22" x 20"
Lent by Grand Lodge of Massachusetts, A.F. & A.M.

Shaped leather apron with painted decoration of quadrant and compasses, pavement and symbols. Inscribed "Time Deum et Patriam Ama" ("Fear God and Love Your Country").

32
MASONIC APRON
Massachusetts, c. 1810-1820
Silk, 16 3/4" x 17"
Lent by Grand Lodge of Massachusetts, A.F. & A.M.

Shaped, white silk apron painted with pillars, mosaic pavement and symbols. Blue silk ribbon border. Belonged to "Bro. Joseph Wells."

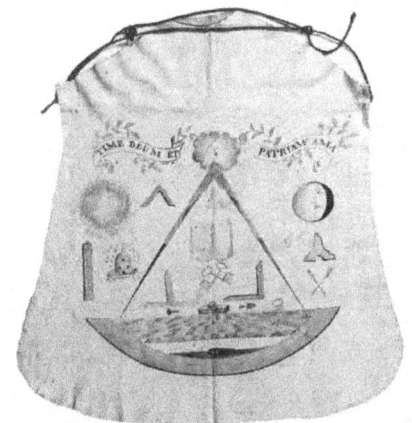

31

33
MASONIC APRON
Danvers, Massachusetts, c. 1823
Silk, 14 1/2" x 14 1/2"
Lent by Essex Institute

White silk apron painted with an all-seeing eye on the flap and a rising sun. Belonged to Samuel P. Fowler of Danvers, Massachusetts, who was admitted to Jordan Lodge, March 26, 1823.

34
MASONIC APRON
O. Eddy, c. 1814-1822
Silk, 15"x 12 1/2"
Lent by Grand Lodge of Massachusetts, A.F. & A.M.

White silk brocade printed with Masonic pillars, carpet and symbols. Blue silk ribbon border. The artist, O. Eddy, is probably Oliver T. Eddy, the son of Isaac Eddy, a Vermont printer and engraver. Born in 1799, Oliver Eddy began engraving in his father's printing establishment as early as 1814. A map of New Hampshire dated "Walpole (N.H.) Aug. 1817" is signed "O.T. Eddy, engraver" (Mantle Fielding, *Dictionary of American Painters*, J. F. Carr, New York, 1965). Eddy left New England sometime before

34

1822 and subsequently lived in Newburgh, New York City, Elizabeth and Newark, New Jersey, Baltimore, and Philadelphia. He worked until his death in 1868 as an artist and inventor. This particular apron was probably engraved in his father's shop between 1814 and 1816.

35
MASONIC APRON
Ashfield, Massachusetts, 1825
Cotton, 15 3/8" x 15 3/4"
Lent by Grand Lodge of Massachusetts, A.F. & A.M.

A white cotton apron appliqued with blue silk and embroidered design of pillars, eye, square and compasses, and "G". Worn by the Master of Morning Sun Lodge, Ashfield, Massachusetts, in 1825.

36
MASONIC APRON
E. Horsman, Boston, Massachusetts c. 1790
Sicl, 17" x 15½"
Museum of Our National Heritage Collection

White silk apron printed with pillars, arch, pavement and symbols, and hand colored with gold. Printed inscription reads, "Master Mason's Apron or Flooring/Copy Right secured/E. Horsman Pinx."

The terms "flooring" and "tracing board" were often used interchangeably, and possibly this engraving was also printed on handkerchiefs that were used as tracing cloths.

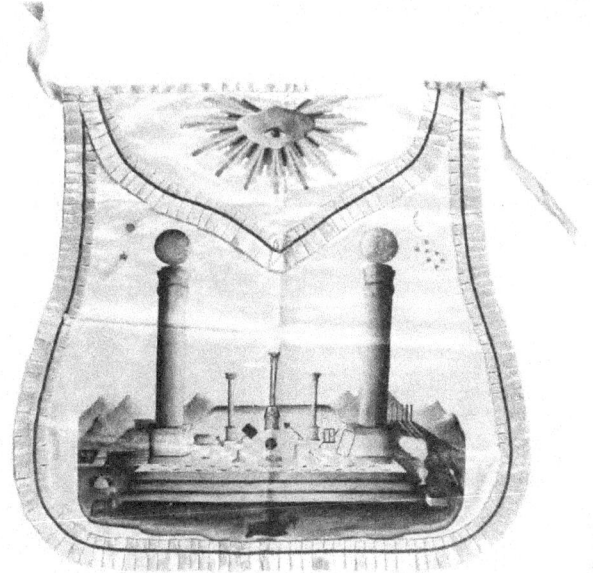

37.
DECANTERS
Bohemian, c. 1790-1810
Glass, 11⅜" high
Lent by Mark Hollander

A pair of taper-shape glass decanters with a band of cut fluting at the neck and base. The copper wheel engraving is a wreath and bow enclosing the Masonic symbols of a triangle, square, compasses, sun and moon, and tools. Both the form and engraved decoration of the decanters match the patterns in a glass catalog dating around 1800, now in the collection of the Henry Francis du Pont Winterthur Museum Libraries. Two catalogs with drawings of glass patterns captioned in German were discovered on Gardiner's Island, New York, where they have a long history of ownership. The name "Johannes Schiefner," which appears on an accompanying price list, has been tentatively associated with a Bohemian glass works, but the American merchant who used the catalogs is not known (Dwight Lanmon, "The Baltimore Glass Trade," *Winterthur Portfolio 5*, The Henry Francis du Pont Winterthur Museum, 1969).

38
TUMBLER
John Frederick Amelung, New Bremen, Maryland, 1785-1795
Glass, 8" high x 5 1/2" diam.
Lent by Connecticut Historical Society

A presentation tumbler engraved with the initials "L.S." and the Masonic symbols of the all-seeing eye, sun, blazing star and moon, square, compasses, trowel, mallet, and level. The attribution to Amelung's glass factory is based on the smoky greenish tint of the glass and the style of the engraving ("Amelung Find—and Puzzle," *Antiques*, Sept. 1964)

Amelung's membership in the fraternity is quite definite. He was reportedly the chief organizer of a lodge in Frederick County, Maryland, near his glass works around 1790 (Edward T. Schultz, *Freemasonry in Maryland*, J.H. Medairt & Co., Baltimore, 1884, v. 1 p. 72).

It is not known who the initials "L.S." stand for. One suggestion has been a member of the Stanger family of the Glassboro, New Jersey, glassworks. Another piece of glass attributed to Amelung is a bottle engraved "F. Stenger" (1792) for Francis Stanger. The reverse of the bottle is engraved with a bottle for his occupation, the plow, represented on the State seal of New Jersey, and the trowel and square for a Freemason (McKearin, *200 years of American Blown Glass*, p. 328).

37

38

39
FIRING GLASS
Possibly U.S., c. 1790-1810
Glass, 4 7/16" x 2 5/16" diam.
Lent by Corning Museum of Glass

Free blown, tooled, and engraved. Medallion of leaf sprays encloses the initials, "F.C.W." Masonic symbols of the square, plumb, trowel, and mallet.

40
FIRING GLASS
Probably Germany, c. 1790-1810
Glass, 4 3/8" x 2 5/8"
Lent by Corning Museum of Glass

Free blown, tooled, and engraved. Solid bottom contains a large tear. Masonic symbols of trowel, moon, sun, mallet, compasses, square, level, triangle and either cable tow or serpent. Emblems are within a U-shaped wreath below the inscription, "Silentio-De-Fiede."

41
WINE GLASS
England, c. 1780
Glass, 4 3/16" x 2" diam.
Lent by Corning Museum of Glass

Free blown, lead glass with applied stem with spirals. Engraved with Masonic symbols of compasses, level, plumb, square, trowel, chisel and mallet. Reverse is engraved with "G" within a star.

42
DECANTER
Possibly Pittsburgh, early 19th century, 10"
Lent by Corning Museum of Glass

Free blown and cut lead glass with 3 triple ring collars and cut decoration of pillars and arches. Within one arch is a square and compasses, stars in the others.

43
TUMBLER
Probably English or German, c. 1790-1810, 3 1/2" x 3 1/4" diam.
Lent by D. Roger Howlett

Blown glass with engraved decoration. Main design of all-seeing eye, sun, moon and stars, with pavement, arch, pillars, square, compasses, "G" and symbols of the Bible, crossed pens and crossed keys, all within a circle with a bow at the top. Reverse engraved with level, plumb, mallet, rule, trowel, and past master's quadrant within a rayed circle. Engraved initials of "W.M.S." This glass has a history of ownership in Connecticut.

44
FIRING GLASS
Probably Germany, c. 1790-1810, 4" x 3" diam.
Lent by D. Roger Howlett

Blown and engraved glass. Design of trowel, moon, sun, mallet, compasses, square, level, triangle and either cable tow or serpent, and is almost identical to the design of 40. The shapes of the two glasses are rather different, however: 40 has a straight cone-shaped bowl and stepped base; 44 has a single disc for a base and a flared bowl.

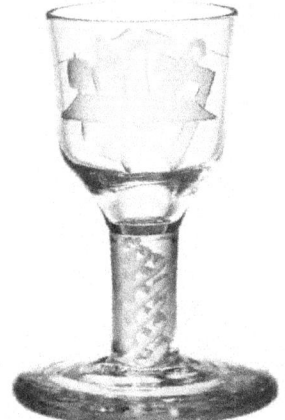

41

45
FLASK
Marlboro Street Works, Keene, New Hampshire, c. 1815-1830
Blown 2 mold glass, 7 1/2"
Museum of Our National Heritage Collection

Olive amber flask with a single rib. Obverse has Masonic pavement, arch and pillars containing the all-seeing eye, radiant triangle, Bible, square and compasses. To the left are the symbols of the blazing star and crossbones. Reverse is the American eagle facing left with arrows in its left talon, olive branch in the right talon. A ribbon above the eagle and plain oval frame below with the inscription "KCCNC" (Keene). (McKearin GIV-19, George S. & Helen McKearin, *American Glass*, Crown Publishers, New York, 1948).

46
FLASK
Probably Marlboro St. Works, Keene, N. H., c. 1815-1830
Blown 2 mold glass, 7 1/2"
Museum of Our National Heritage Collection

Light green flask with five vertical ribs. Obverse has Masonic pavement, arch and pillars containing all-seeing eye, open Bible and square and compasses, and radiant triangle with the letter "G". To the left are the symbols of the blazing sun, trowel, skull and crossbones, and scythe. At the right are the crescent moon surrounded by seven stars, a comet with a tail. Below pavement at right is the beehive. The obverse is the American eagle turned to the left with a shield of bars and dots on its breast. Three arrows in its left talon, olive branch in its right. Plain ribbon above the eagle, and oval beaded frame containing "NEG Co" below. Although the initials undoubtedly stand for New England Glass Co., it is quite likely that the flask was made at Keene for the New England Glass Co. (McKearin GIV-27).

47
FLASK
Marlboro St. Works, Keene, New Hampshire, c. 1815-1830
Blown 2 mold glass, 6"
Lent by Sandwich Glass Museum

Amber flask with single vertical rib. Obverse has Masonic pavement, arch and pillars containing all-seeing eye, open Bible with square and compasses, and triangle (McKearin GIV-25). The reverse is the American eagle with head turned to the right holding balls in its talons. A plain ribbon is above the eagle, and a plain oval below. This corresponds with the design of McKearin GIV-24 rather than GIV-25.

48
FLASK
Marlboro St. Works, Keene, New Hampshire, c. 1815-1830
Blown 2 mold glass, 7 1/2"
Lent by Sandwich Glass Museum

Clear green flask with five vertical ribs. Obverse has the Masonic pavement, arch and pillars containing all-seeing eye, open Bible with the square and compasses, and radiant triangle enclosing the letter "G". To the left is the radiant sun, trowel, and skull and crossbones. To the right is the moon, stars, and ladder. Beneath the pavement is the crossed level and plumb to the left, and the beehive to the right. The reverse is the American Eagle turned to the left with a shield of horizontal and vertical bars on its breast. It holds three arrows in its left talon and the olive branch in its right. The ribbon above the eagle is inscribed "E PLURIBUS UNUM" and the oval frame below is inscribed "IP" for Justus Perry. (McKearin GIV-1).

48

49
FLASK
Marlboro St. Works, Keene, New Hampshire, c. 1815-1830
Blown 3 mold glass, 7 1/4"
Lent by Grand Lodge of Massachusetts, A.F. & A.M.

Clear green flask with five vertical ribs and wide mouth. Obverse has same Masonic design as 48 above. Reverse is similar except that the shield on the eagle has tiny dots instead of horizontal bars, and the beaded oval frame contains an eight-pointed star (McKearin GIV-5).

50
FLASK
White Glass Works, Zanesville, Ohio, c. 1815-1830
Blown 2 mold glass, 6 1/2"
Lent by Grand Lodge of Massachusetts, A.F. & A.M.

Aquamarine flask with vertical ribbing. Obverse has Masonic pavement, arch and pillars containing the "Farmer's Arms" of a sheaf of rye, pitchfork, rake, sickle, etc. Obverse is the American eagle turned to the right with shield of seven bars on its breast. Five arrows in its right talon, olive branch in the left. Eagle stands on a beaded oval frame enclosing "Ohio." "Zanesville" inscribed in semi-circle above eagle, "J. Shepard & Co." below the eagle (McKearin GIV-32).

51
FLASK
Kensington Glass Works, Philadelphia, c. 1815-1830
Blown 2 mold glass, 6 1/2"
Lent by Grand Lodge of Massachusetts, A.F. & A.M.

Pale green flask with vertical ribbing. Obverse has Masonic pavement, arch, pillars, and Farmer's Arms similar to 50 above. Obverse has American Eagle turned to the right with shield of seven bars on its breast. It holds five arrows in its right talons, olive branch in its left. Eagle stands on beaded oval frame with initials, "T.W.D." (McKearin GIV-37).

52

52
FLASK
Pittsburgh district, c. 1850's
Blown 2 mold glass, 8 3/4"
Lent by Grand Lodge of Massachusetts, A.F. & A.M.

Aquamarine flask. Obverse is a shield with clasped hands in a scalloped frame above the square and compasses and five five-pointed stars. Above the shield is the inscription "UNION" and a semicircle of stars, and below the shield is an olive branch. The reverse is an American eagle perched on a shield, arrows and olive branch. Oval frame below the eagle is inscribed "H. & S." (McKearin GIV-39).

53
FLASK
A.R. Samuels, Kensington Glass Works, Philadelphia, c. 1850's
Blown 2 mold glass, 8 1/2"
Lent by Grand Lodge of Massachusetts, A.F. & A.M.

Aquamarine calabash shape flask with fluted edges. Similar design to 52 above (McKearin GIV-42).

The McKearins suggest an association with the Junior Order of United American Mechanics although these two flasks are included in the Masonic category because of the symbols. Additional evidence, however, points to another American patriotic and nativist society, the Brotherhood of the Union, founded in Philadelphia in 1850. The following quotation, taken from a published paper of the organization, states that, "The spirit of the order is expressed in the word 'Union'—union of the good against evil; union of the just against the unjust..." (Albert C. Stevens, *Cyclopaedia of Fraternities*, Hamilton Printing and Publishing Co., New York, 1899, p. 300). With other patriotic secret societies of this period, the Brotherhood of the Union was a component of the Know Nothing party of the 1850's. Like many other fraternal societies, it probably borrowed the symbols of Freemasonry for its insignia. The use of the word "union" and the fact that both of these flasks were made in Pennsylvania where the Brotherhood's main strength was concentrated, strongly support the connection between this flask design and the Brotherhood of the Union during the Know Nothing political period of the 1850's.

54
FLASK
Thomas Stebbins, Coventry, Connecticut, c. 1824
Blown 2 mold glass, 7 1/2"
Lent by Corning Museum of Glass

Amber flask with horizontal corrugations along edge. Obverse has profile of Lafayette, facing right, and inscription "LAFAYETTE" in semicircle above bust; "T.S." in bar below. Reverse is Masonic pavement, arch and pillars containing triangle and open Bible, sun to the left and moon to the right (McKearin GI-83).

55
FLASK
Mount Vernon Glass Works, Vernon, New York, c. 1824
Blown 2 mold glass, 6 1/2"
Lent by Corning Museum of Glass

Deep olive green flask with single vertical rib. Obverse has profile facing right with inscription "LAFAYETTE" above. Reverse is Masonic pavement, arch and pillars containing triangle and open Bible with square and compasses (McKearin GI-89).

56
FLASK
Knox & McKee, Wheeling, West Virginia, c. 1824
Blown 2 mold glass, 7 1/4"
Lent by Corning Museum of Glass

Clear green flask. Obverse has a profile turned to the right with the arch and pillars above and a fleur de lis below, and the inscription, "GENL LA FAYETTE" in semicircle along lower edges. Reverse has the American eagle turned to the left holding two arrows and olive branch, with six cannon balls below and seven five-pointed stars above eagle. "WHEELING" inscribed in semicircle along upper edge, "KNOX & MCKEE" along lower edge (McKearin GI-93).

57
FLASK
Kensington Glass Works, Philadelphia, c. 1815-1830
Blown 2 mold glass, 6 3/4"
Lent by Corning Museum of Glass

Deep amber flask with vertical ribbing along edges. Obverse has Masonic pavement, arch and pillars, enclosing the "Farmer's Arms." Scroll ornament below and inscription "KENSINGTON GLASS WORKS PHILADELPHIA" along outer edge. Reverse is a full-rigged frigate with American flag and the inscription "FRANKLIN" in semicircle below. "FREE TRADE AND SAILOR'S RIGHTS" inscribed around outer edge (McKearin GIV-34).

58

58
FLASK
Kensington Glass Works, Philadelphia, c. 1815-1830
Blown 2 mold glass, 6 1/2"
Lent by Corning Museum of Glass

Aquamarine flask, identical to 57 above without the inscriptions along the edges (McKearin GIV-35).

**59
COVERLET**
Attributed to James Alexander, Orange County, New York, 1830
Wool and cotton, 96" x 72"
Museum of Our National Heritage Collection

Blue and white double woven Jacquard coverlet with center seam and border design of Masonic pillars, square and compasses, Independence Hall, liberty bell and eagle, and the inscription, "AGRICULTURE AND MANUFACTURES ARE THE FOUNDATION OF OUR INDEPENDENCE/HULDAH PENNY JULY 4, 1830."

**60
JUG**
c. 1870
Stoneware, 17 1/2" high
Museum of Our National Heritage Collection

Salt glazed stoneware with cobalt blue freehand decoration of Masonic square, compasses, and "G", and the inscription "C. Damon."

61
JAR
Justin Campbell, Utica, New York, 1823
Stoneware, 13 1/2" high
Lent by New York State Historical Association

Salt glazed stoneware jar with incised decoration of square and compasses, trowel, mallet, plumb, and apron, filled with blue glaze. Inscribed "P. Darrow/of Rome/N. York/1823." Impressed mark, "J. Campbell/Utica."

62
JUG
West Troy Pottery, West Troy, New York, c. 1870
Stoneware, 16 1/2" high
Lent by Mr. and Mrs. Charles V. Hagler

Salt glazed stoneware with cobalt blue freehand decoration of Masonic square, compasses, and "G". Impressed mark, "West Troy Pottery."

63
LANTERN
Early 19th century
Pierced tin, 13" x 5 1/4" diam.
Lent by Mr. and Mrs. Charles V. Hagler

Pierced tin lantern with designs of square and compasses and crossed keys.

64
COVERLET
New York State, c. 1830-40
Wool and cotton, 90" x 76"
Lent by Foster McCarl Jr.

Blue and white double woven Jacquard coverlet with center seam. Border of Masonic symbols includes the eye, star, pavement, anchor and beehive, as well as the working tools of Masons. The trowel, and square and compasses, are also worked into the medallions of the center design.

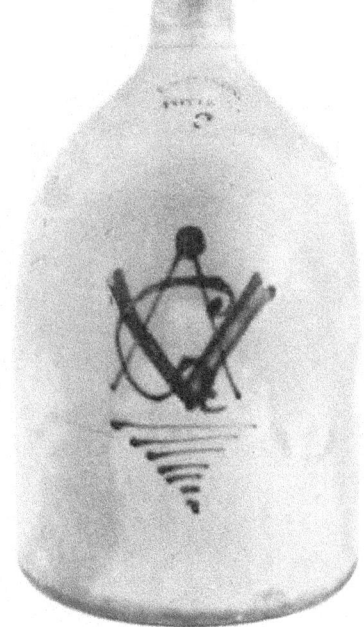

62

64

69

65
LONGRIFLE
Attributed to Andrew Verner, Bethlehem, Reading area of Pennsylvania, c. 1815
Lent by John Hamilton

Pennsylvania longrifle with incised carved stock and engraved brass patchbox. The 14 brass inlays include a double headed eagle for which Andrew Verner was noted. The tail of the upper ramrod pipe is engraved with the compasses and mallet.

66
SWORD
United States, c. 1810
Silver, 37 1/2"
Lent by the Essex Institute

A U.S. Infantry Officer's sword with a cut and thrust blade and reeded ivory grip. The unmarked silver hilt has a pillow pommel, five ball knuckle guard, and square and compasses pierced in positive silhouette within the sidearm.

67
POWDER HORN
Kentucky, 1769, Horn, 10"
Lent by the Supreme Council, Ancient and Accepted Scottish Rite of Freemasonry, Southern Jurisdiction

Engraved powder horn with Masonic symbols of the past master's square, compasses and quadrant, and the figure of a man smoking a pipe. Inscribed, "N. Haddix."

68
POWDER HORN
New York, 1772, Horn, 12"
Lent by Supreme Council, Ancient and Accepted Scottish Rite of Freemasonry, Southern Jurisdiction

Engraved powder horn that belonged to Robert Yates of New York. The engraved decoration includes a map of New York State, a view of New York City, Masonic symbols, and the inscriptions, "Don't tread on me," and "MASONRY LIKE POWDER AND BALL NOBELL LIKE DOTH LEVEL ALL."

69
POWDER HORN
1817
Horn, 12"
Lent by Chicago Historical Society

Engraved powder horn with animals, Masonic symbols and the inscriptions, "Don't tread on me", and "Death or Liberty 1817".

70
WALLPAPER
Groton, Massachusetts, c. 1800
Lent by Old Sturbridge Village

A fragment of original wallpaper dating from c. 1800 that was removed from a building located in Groton, Mass. The design consists of the pillars, arch and "G," and a man wearing a Masonic apron.

72

71
SECRETARY
Massachusetts, late 18th century
Mahogany and maple, 49 1/2" high x 38 1/2" x 19 1/2"
Lent by Old Sturbridge Village

Mahogany Hepplewhite secretary with inlaid design of the square and compasses on the hinged doors.

72
CHAIR
American, 1788
Mahogany and cherry, 39" x 20 3/4"
Lent by Portland Museum of Art, Purchase Jewell Fund, 1975

Chippendale side chair with carved crest of Masonic square and compasses. One of a set made as a wedding present for Captain Joseph McLellan, Jr., of Portland, Maine.

73

75
TAVERN SIGN
H. Page, Coventry, Connecticut, before 1822
Painted wood, 33 3/4" x 23"
Lent by the Connecticut Historical Society

Shield shaped tavern sign painted with a man holding a bird, and two birds in a bush with the Masonic square & compasses below. Inscribed "H. Rose/A bird in the hand is worth /two in the bush," and signed, "H. Page." The history of the sign is that it was taken down in 1822 when the former tavern was used as a private home.

73
CUT PAPER PICTURE
c. 1850
Paper, 12 1/2" x 14"
Lent by Mr. and Mrs. Charles V. Hagler

Cut paper picture with design of a cat standing at the bottom of a tree filled with birds on each side of an altar with cupids and the Masonic square and compasses; two ladies holding parasols standing at the base. Done on lined paper, this was probably a piece of schoolgirl art.

74
TRIVET
Late 18th century
Brass, 8" x 3 5/8"
Lent by Mr. and Mrs. Charles V. Hagler

Cast brass trivet with pierced design of square, compasses, pillars, moon, stars, and heart.

74

77
GRAVESTONE RUBBING
Groton, Massachusetts, 1821
Peper, 54" x 33 1/2"
Lent by Mr. and Mrs. Fred R. Youngren

Rubbing taken from the gravestone of Mr. Alpheus Richardson. The carved design of this stone reflects the classicism of the period and a shift in the style of gravestone decoration. The design consists of pillars topped with classical urns and an arch with the "G" in the keystone. The arch is surmounted by a willow and urn, characteristic designs on gravestones of this period. The Masonic symbols of the spade, plumb, level, square and compasses, mallet, rule, and trowel are arranged in a semicircle within the arch.

77

78

76
GRAVESTONE RUBBING
Shrewsbury, Massachusetts, 1793
Paper, 54" x 33 1/2"
Lent by Mr. and Mrs. Fred R. Youngren

Rubbing taken from the gravestone of Major John Farrar. The carved design of the stone includes the square, compasses and Bible, the all-seeing eye, sun, moon, and star, mallet and trowel, sprig of acacia, coffin, and the number 15.

78
JAMES MADISON WINN WEARING MASONIC CUFFLINKS
Newburyport, Massachusetts, c. 1850's
Oil on canvas, 30" x 20"
Lent by the Essex Institute

One of a pair of portraits of Winn and his wife done by an unknown artist. Winn was a shoemaker in Newburyport, Massachusetts, and lived from 1830 to 1877.

79
WORSHIPFUL MASTER'S CHAIR
John Luker, Vinton County, Ohio, c. 1870
Pine and maple, 72" x 29 1/4" x 30"
Lent by Mr. and Mrs. Charles V. Hagler

Worshipful Master's Chair painted with Masonic symbols and inscribed, "Manufact'd by John Luker" and "J.H.M. Houston." Houston was the Worshipful Master of Swan Lodge No. 358 located in Swan, Ohio, near Mount Pleasant in Vinton County, Ohio. The lodge was chartered in 1866 and Houston was Worshipful Master from 1867 to 1873. A new building for the lodge was dedicated in 1871, and it is probable that the chair was made at that time. Although there is no record of John Luker's being a Mason, it is quite possible that the Joseph Luker who was initiated into Swan Lodge in 1870 was his relative.

80
COLUMNS AND CANDLESTICKS
Vinton County, Ohio, c. 1870
Painted wood, 68" and 32" high
Lent by Mr. and Mrs. Charles V. Hagler

Columns and candlesticks of the same Swan Lodge No. 358, Ohio, and probably made by John Luker who made the Worshipful Master's Chair.

Masonic Lodge Building, Mt. Pleasant, Ohio.

81
THE BOGOTA
China, c. 1850
Oil on canvas, 17 1/2" x 24"
Lent by Mr. and Mrs. Gerald Knicely

Chinese export painting of the American brig, "Bogota" entering Hong Kong harbor. The tradition of using Masonic flags at sea among American, English, and other European nations dates at least to the 1840's and '50's. The flag was used as a distress signal or recognition inquiry at sea, and in port was an invitation for other Masonic Captains to share the ship's hospitality. In 1863, the Grand Lodges of Europe suggested the adoption of a French Masonic flag of a blue field with a Masonic square and compasses in a white circle, to be used for friendly recognition or distress. An article in the "Freemasons' Monthly Magazine" of Boston for August, 1863, documents the earlier use of Masonic flags, describing an "old Masonic flag with the square and compasses," probably similar to the flag on the "Bogota" with a blue field and white symbol.

The author of the 1863 item, Hyde Clark, Deputy Grand Master for Turkey, relates that this Masonic flag was "used extensively by the English, American, and Northern maritime nations and in this part of Asia we see it frequently" (Transactions of the American Lodge of Research, Volume III, No. 1, p. 163).

82
CHEST
c. 1800-1820
Pine, 17" x 40" x 18"
Museum of Our National Heritage Collection

Pine chest painted red and stenciled with black design of Masonic arch, columns, and Masonic square and compasses on the front; the arch, columns, sun and alpha, and moon and omega on the ends. The stenciled initials, "M. W." could be personal initials but more likely are "Most Worshipful." The chest was probably used in a lodge to store Masonic regalia. The proceedings of the Grand Lodge of Massachusetts for December 12, 1796 mention a vote "to procure a trunk and columns for the use of the Grand Lodge." Masonic lodges of this period were sometimes decorated with painted or stenciled wall decorations and it is interesting to speculate whether the chest might have been used in a room with similar decorations.

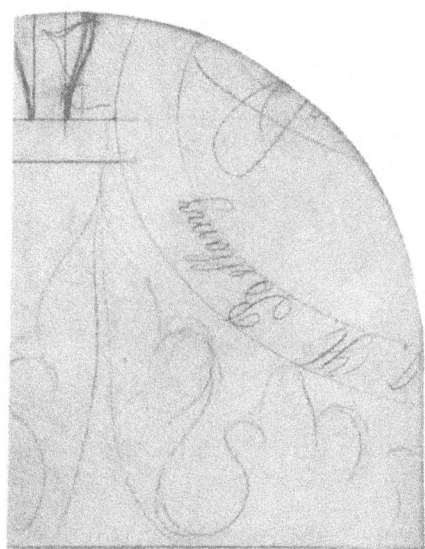

83
FRAME
J.H. Bellamy, Massachusetts, or Maine, c. 1868
Wood, 32" x 22"
Lent by H. Sterling French

Carved frame with Masonic symbols made for the Masonic certificate of George W. Southworth of Lynn, Massachusetts, dated 1868. The certificate was backed with a pattern which includes the name, "J.H. Bellamy." John Haley Bellamy was a wood carver in Maine, Portsmouth, New Hampshire, and Boston. Although he is best known for his ship figureheads and carved eagles, he also carved decorative pieces and family coats of arms. Heraldry was a hobby of his and his familiarity with the subject is obvious in the design of this frame. The Masonic symbols have been cleverly arranged to simulate armorial devices. The trowel forms a shield and the level has been treated like a camail, or chain mail hood in armor (Victor Stafford, *ANTIQUES*, March 1935).

84
CARVED WHALE TOOTH
19th century, 6"
Lent by the Supreme Council, Ancient and Accepted Scottish Rite of Freemasonry, Southern Jurisdiction

Carving in relief of quadrant, compasses and "G" enclosed in a wreath.

85
BOX
Possibly England, c. 1812
Bone, 2 7/8" x 1 5/16"
Museum of Our National Heritage Collection

Small bone box with hinged lid, and decorated with prisoner of war type carving from the period of the War of 1812. Carving in relief of Masonic pillars, arch, and symbols of the all-seeing eye, square and compasses, Bible and altar, sun and moon, and spade and gavel.

86
LIVERPOOL PITCHER
England, c. 1790
Ceramic, 10"
Lent by Dr. and Mrs. Oscar Hollander

Transfer printed creamware pitcher with the American ship, "Robert Burns" on obverse. Reverse is a standard Masonic pattern signed "Kennedy" for James Kennedy, a Burslem, England, engraver. The design consists of the two pillars, J. and B., surmounted by the two wardens, a central column with the master's square, and the mosaic pavement. These are surrounded by sprays of flowers and leaves and topped by the symbol of charity, a mother and children. Within the columns are the Masonic symbols of the all-seeing eye, sun, moon and stars, crossed keys, crossed pens, star, acacia, Euclid's problem, apron, Bible, square and compasses, ladder, three candlesticks and coffin. Under the spout are the initials, "H I C" within a wreath of flowers, leaves, wheat, and barrels topped by a wine glass.

87
LIVERPOOL PITCHER
England, 1811
Ceramic, 11"
Museum of Our National Heritage Collection
Gift of Union Lodge, A.F. & A.M., Dorchester, Massachusetts

A pair of transfer printed creamware pitchers presented to Union Lodge in 1811 by Nehemiah Skillings. The obverse is the standard Masonic pattern most commonly found on Liverpool pitchers imported to America. The design consists of two pillars and the mosaic pavement, surrounded by floral and leaf sprays and surmounted by the figures of Faith, Hope, and Charity. Between the columns are the Masonic symbols of the sun, moon and stars, all-seeing eye, level, plumb and trowel, Bible, square and compasses, crossed pens, pick and shovel, maul, crossed keys, Euclid's problem, hour glass, acacia, coffin, star and "G", cock, beehive, and three candlesticks. The reverse is an oval engraving with the inscription, "Veritas Prevalebit" (the truth will prevail) illustrating an event in Masonic lore. The transfer under the spout is the insignia of the Royal Arch Chapter of England before 1817 and the inscriptions, "Cemented with Love" and "Holiness to the Lord," both identified with Royal Arch Masonry. The name "Union Lodge" appears under the Royal Arch insignia.

88
LIVERPOOL PITCHER
England, c. 1790-1810
Ceramic, 11"
Lent by the Peabody Museum of Salem

Transfer printed creamware pitcher. The obverse is printed with the same standard design as 87 above, and the inscription, "Lodge No. 25." The reverse is a ship flying the American flag and the inscription "The Three Sisters." The transfers under the spout are the name "P. Delano" within a floral and grape wreath, and the square, compasses and "G". Around the mouth is a border of floral sprays.

Aut Mori/Success to the Independent Boston Fusiliers, Incorporated July 4, 1787. America forever." The reverse is an engraving with three allegorical figures including Liberty and Justice, and the inscription, "United We Stand & Divided We Fall." Above this engraving and under the spout is a transfer design of the eagle of the United States seal.

Samuel Jenks was first initiated into the Masonic fraternity in 1760, in the military lodge at Fort Frederick during the Crown Point campaign. He was also a member of King Solomon's Lodge, Charlestown, Massachusetts, from 1796. Mentioned in the Grand Lodge of Massachusetts Proceedings, the "Independent Fusileers" led the procession at the Masonic celebration of laying the cornerstone of the new State House, Boston, on July 4, 1795.

90
LIVERPOOL PITCHER
England, c. 1790-1810
Ceramic, 9 3/4"
Lent by the Grand Lodge of Massachusetts, A.F. & A.M.

Transfer printed creamware pitcher. The obverse is printed with the same stock design as 86 above. The shapes of these two pitchers are also alike. The reverse is the inscription,

Hail, Masonry divine!
Glory of ages shine,
Long may'st thou reign!
Where'er thy Lodges stand,
And always grace the land,
Thou Art divine!

surrounded by a wreath of floral sprays and Masonic symbols. This engraving is also signed "Kennedy." The initials "T R," in a wreath, are under the spout.

89
LIVERPOOL PITCHER
England, 1790
Ceramic, 9 1/2"
Lent by the Peabody Museum of Salem

Transfer printed creamware pitcher. One hundred of these pitchers were made by special order of Samuel Jenks in 1790, and presented to each member of the Boston Fusiliers. The design on the obverse consists of a uniformed fusilier standing on a black and white pavement with distinct Masonic connections. Above the oval framing him are the Masonic symbols of the all-seeing eye, sun, moon and stars, the square, compasses and "G", and the level. Perhaps the symbol of the level was specifically used here to emphasize the equality of all members of the company. The inscription around the oval frame is "Aut Vincere

91
LIVERPOOL PITCHER
England, c. 1802
Ceramic, 11" high
Lent by the Grand Lodge of Massachusetts, A.F. & A.M.

Transfer printed creamware pitcher. The obverse is a ship design and the reverse is the standard Masonic design found on 87 above. Under the spout are the initials "E B H" and the transfer design of the eagle of the United States seal. This pitcher belonged to Captain Ebenezer B. Hatch who was passed and raised a Master Mason in Mount Lebanon Lodge in Boston on January 29, 1802. His Masonic records show that he was a master mariner and also lived in Gorham, Maine.

92
LIVERPOOL PITCHER
England, 1796-1803
Ceramic, 8 1/2"
Lent by the Grand Lodge of Massachusetts, A.F. & A.M.

Transfer printed creamware pitcher. Obverse is printed with a patriotic design of interlocking rings representing 16 states including Kentucky and Tennessee, which dates this design between 1796 and 1803. The eagle of the United States seal within the rings, the American flag and liberty cap above. The reverse is the standard Masonic design found on 87 above. The design under the spout is a sentimental engraving showing a young woman offering a butterfly to a young man, and the inscription "Friendship Love and Unity/Accept this Pledge of Affection."

93
LIVERPOOL PITCHER
England, c. 1790-1810
Ceramic, 8 3/4"
Lent by the Grand Lodge of Massachusetts, A.F. & A.M.

Transfer printed creamware pitcher. The design on the obverse is the same as the standard Masonic pattern found on 87. The reverse is a patriotic design of two allegorical figures, with cornucopias, an eagle, and the seal of the United States with the inscription, "Peace Plenty and Independence."

94

**94
MUG**
Ralph Wedgwood, Ferrybridge, England, 1796-1800
Ceramic, 6 1/4" x 4" diam.
Lent by Essex Institute

Transfer printed creamware mug with the impressed mark, "WEDGWOOD & CO." of Ralph Wedgwood, a manufacturer of stoneware and creamware. The transfer design is a version of the Freemason's Arms and the mottoes: "Amor Honor et Justitia" associated with the "Moderns" in England, and "The Heart that Conceals and the Tongue that Never Reveals." The mug has a history of ownership by the Curwen family of Salem, Massachusetts.

**95
BOWL**
England, c. 1796-1800
Ceramic, 4 1/2" x 10 1/2" diam.
Lent by the Albany Institute of History and Art

Transfer printed creamware bowl with the same design of the Freemason's Arms and the same mottoes as 94. Other transfers around the sides of the bowl include hunting and agricultural subjects. Possibly made by the same company although not marked.

**96
LIVERPOOL PITCHER**
England, c. 1790-1810
Ceramic, 7 7/8"
Lent by the Grand Lodge of Massachusetts, A.F. & A.M.

Transfer printed creamware pitcher. Obverse has design of all-seeing eye, sun, moon and stars, and the square, compasses, and "G". Reverse consists of an oval with a border of triangles and Masonic symbols. Design within the oval is made up of two columns and globes, and the mosaic pavement. Above the columns are the eye, sun, moon and stars. Between them are the square, compasses, "G", sword, rule, trowel, Bible, and three candlesticks. On either side of the columns are the symbols of the gavel, plumb, mallet, key, apron and hour glass, and the ladder, level, rule and compasses, and the coffin. Under the spout is the inscription, "Virtue is the chiefest Beauty of the Mind/The Noblest ornament of Humankind."

96

97
LIVERPOOL PITCHER
England, c. 1790-1810
Ceramic, 10 1/2"
Museum of Our National Heritage Collection
Gift of Mrs. Fred H. Barrows, Jr.

Transfer printed creamware pitcher. Obverse printed with the same design as 87. Reverse is printed with a verse of the Entered Apprentice's Song:

The World is in Pain
Our Secrets to gain.
But still let them wonder & gaze on.
For they ne'er can divine
The WORD or the SIGN.
Of a Free and Accepted Mason.

Under the spout are the initials, "W N T" in a wreath of Masonic symbols, and the square, compasses and "G" below. Under the handle is a transfer of a Royal Arch symbol.

98
LIVERPOOL PITCHER
England, c. 1804
Ceramic, 9"
Lent by the Grand Lodge of Massachusetts, A.F. & A.M.

Transfer printed and colored creamware pitcher. Obverse is the same standard design as 87 except that the inscription, "United for the Benefit of Mankind" is added below. The reverse is a transfer engraving of a mother and children, representing Charity, surrounded by the arch, pillars, three steps, and all-seeing eye of Freemasonry. The inscription reads:

To judge with candor, and to speak no wrong
The feeble to support, against the strong
To soothe the wretched, and the poor to feed
Will cover many an idle foolish deed

The transfer under the spout is the eagle of the United States seal and the inscription, "Peace, Commerce, and honest Friendship with all Nations—Entangling Alliances with none. JEFFERSON./Anno Domini 1804."

99
PITCHER
England, c. 1809
Ceramic, 7 1/4" x 7 1/2" diam.
Lent by the Grand Lodge of Massachusetts, A.F. & A.M.

Hand decorated "gaudy" earthenware with luster band at the base. Obverse inscribed, "Ferguson & Euphemia McDonald." Under the spout is a square and compasses and a plane, gouge, and turning tool for threading screws, probably indicating that McDonald was a woodworker by trade. Reverse painted with floral decoration.

99

99

100
PITCHER
England, c. 1810-1830
Ceramic, 8 1/2"
Lent by Mr. and Mrs. Charles V. Hagler

Sunderland luster pitcher with printed designs. Obverse is "A West View of the Iron Bridge over the Wear under the Patronage of R. Burdon Esqr. M.P." Reverse is a rectangular design of the two columns and globes and allegorical figures of Justice and Beauty on either side of a building. The all-seeing eye above and Masonic symbols of the ladder, beehive, square, level, crossed pens and keys, and compasses arranged around the edges. The Entered Apprentice's Song, "The World is in pain. . ." (see 97) appears in an oval between the columns. Under the spout is the inscription, in a floral wreath:

> Swiftly See Each Moment Flies,
> See and Learn Be Timely Wise,
> Every Pulse Beats Life Away,
> Thus Thy Every Heaving Breath,
> Waft Thee on To Certain Death,
> Seize the Moments As They Fly,
> Know To Live and Learn To Die.

101
PITCHER
England, c. 1830-40
Ceramic, 8"
Museum of Our National Heritage Collection
Gift of Union Lodge, A.F. & A.M., Dorchester, Massachusetts

Purple luster transfer printed earthenware pitcher. Obverse has design made up of three columns topped by the stars, sun, and moon, and joined by a rope from which two medals are suspended. The working tools of Masons are applied to the columns and the symbols of a coffin and tent are also used. The reverse is a figure seated on three steps in front of a beehive and between the two columns topped with globes. The various symbols of Freemasonry are arranged around and include a shield-shaped Freemason's arms. Under the spout is the mother and children depicting Charity.

101

101

102
MUG
England, c. 1830-40
Ceramic, 4 1/4" x 4" diam.
Museum of Our National Heritage Collection
Gift of William D. Mathieson

Light blue transfer printed earthenware with a frog inside. Printed design of columns, globes, pavement, all-seeing eye, Bible, candlesticks, apron, tent, and other symbols repeated twice around mug. Hand painted initials, "A:J:M."

103
PLATE
England, c. 1810-1830
Ceramic, 8 1/2" x 9 1/2"
Lent by the Grand Lodge of Massachusetts, A.F. & A.M.

Copper and pink luster transfer printed with same design as the reverse of 100, including the Entered Apprentice's Song, "The World is in pain..."

104
PLATE
England, 1820-30
Ceramic, 5 1/2" diam.
Lent by Mr. and Mrs. Charles V. Hagler

Creamware plate with Masonic emblems in relief around border and colored with iron-red and green. Center design of hand-painted pot of flowers.

105
PLATE
England, 1820-30
Ceramic, 5 1/2" diam.
Lent by Mr. and Mrs. Charles V. Hagler

Same border as 104, but with center design of landscape and houses.

106
PLATE
England, 1820-30
Ceramic, 7 1/2" diam.
Lent by Mr. and Mrs. Charles V. Hagler

Same border as 104, but with center design of single flower.

107
PITCHER
England, 1820-30
Ceramic, 6"
Lent by Mr. and Mrs. Charles V. Hagler

Polychrome design of figure seated below an arch and columns next to a shield-shaped Freemason's Arms and surrounded by other symbols of Freemasonry. Inscribed, "Industry Providence Love & Truth/The Freemason's Arms." Reverse is the Entered Apprentice's Song, "The World is in pain. . ." (see 97).

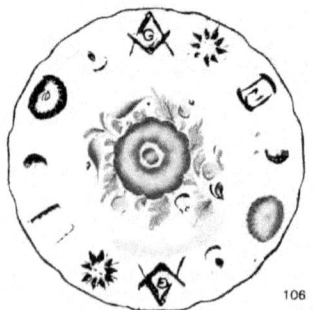

108
PLATE
James and Ralph Clews, Staffordshire, England, c. 1830
Ceramic, 10 1/2" diam.
Museum of Our National Heritage Collection

Blue Staffordshire transfer printed plate in the States Design with a University Building, and the figures of America and Independence. The figure of America, holding a portrait of Washington, wears the blindfold of justice and a Masonic apron.

109

109
COFFEE POT
Chinese Export, c. 1790
Porcelain, 10"
Museum of Our National Heritage Collection

Chinese export lighthouse coffee pot with dome lid and berry finial. Gold monogram design of square and compasses with initials, "R.M.P." Narrow blue and gold border.

110
TEAPOT
Chinese Export, c. 1790-1810
Porcelain, 5 1/2"
Lent by the Albany Institute of History and Art

Chinese export cylindrical teapot with berry finial, gold grapevine border and polychrome symbols. Central design of pillars, globes and pavement, square and compasses, and initials "L.M." in a circular frame topped with a head of wheat. Symbols of the stars, moon, clouds, and sun arranged on either side.

111
MUG
Chinese Export, c. 1800-1820
Porcelain, 5 1/2" x 4 1/4" diam.
Lent by the Lodge of St. Andrew, A.F.&A.M., Boston, Massachusetts

Chinese export mug decorated with polychrome Masonic symbols. Central design of pillars, globes, pavement and "G" within a circular frame topped with a head of wheat. On either side are the symbols of the beehive, a workbench with tools, the square, level, and plumb, a rough ashlar and tools, a protractor and rules, a smooth ashlar, and the square, compasses, and Bible. The border design is a blue field with gold grapevine design. The mug originally belonged to John Suter who lived 1781 to 1852.

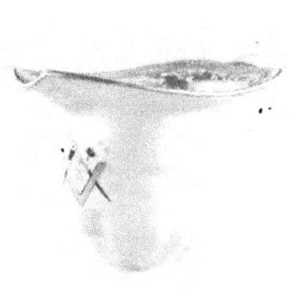

113

112
BOWL
Chinese Export, c. 1820
Porcelain, 5 1/2" x 13 3/8" diam.
Lent by the Albany Institute of History and Art

Chinese export bowl with border of gold stars on a blue field and decorated with polychrome Masonic symbols. Inside of punch bowl has same standard design of pillars and globes in circular frame as the mug above, and the sun, moon, stars, and clouds found on 110. The exterior is decorated with the same symbols as 111.

113
TEA SERVICE
Chinese Export, c. 1815
Porcelain
Private collection

Chinese export tea service consisting of light house coffee pot, cylindrical tea pot, two footed sugar bowls, helmet shaped creamer, waste bowl, cups with handles and saucers, and various sized plates. The design is a gold grapevine border and monogram of the initials "J.S.B." below the square and compasses, sun, moon, stars, trowel, and mallet. The set originally belonged to Jacob Battis of Philadelphia.

114

115
LACQUER BOX
Japan, c. 1830-1840
Lacquer, 4 1/8" x 13 3/4" x 7 3/4"
Museum of Our National Heritage Collection
Gift of Mrs. Norman H. Smith

Black lacquer box inlaid with mother of pearl. Center panel of standard Japanese Masonic design similar to 114, and flanked by two floral panels. Floral designs on the sides.

116

114
CIGAR BOX
Japan, before 1799
Lacquer, 5 1/2" x 3 3/4"
Lent by Carl Crossman

This lacquer box with gold Masonic decoration is one of the earliest documented pieces of Japanese lacquer ware in America. It has a history of having been presented to General Stevens by George Washington, thus dating it before 1799. Direct American trade with Japan dates from 1797-1801 when several American ships were chartered by the Dutch East India Company to fulfill their trade agreement with Japan allowing one Dutch ship a year. Americans were able to resume direct contact after Commodore Perry's negotiations and the opening of Japan to American trade in 1854. Japanese goods, however, reached England and America continuously through trade with the Dutch. Washington may have obtained the box as a gift from one of his Dutch acquaintances like Houkgeest Van Braam, a Dutch merchant sympathetic to American Independence.

The design of symbols includes the pillars and globes, pavement, all-seeing eye, sun, moon, stars, square and compasses, as well as the less common symbols of a Royal Arch temple, and a tent. These two symbols are frequently found on English glassware and ceramics. Since this arrangement of symbols is duplicated on almost every Japanese lacquer box with Masonic symbols of the early 19th century, it would appear that the Japanese used a single prototype for their Masonic design.

116
LACQUER BOX
Japan, mid-19th century
Lacquer, 5" x 16 1/4" x 12 1/2"
Museum of Our National Heritage Collection
Gift of C. Fred Hewitt

Black lacquer box inlaid with mother of pearl design of eye, altar, beehive, hourglass, compasses, square, clasped hands, and trowel. Floral designs around sides.

117
ALBUM QUILT
Staten Island, New York., early 1900's
Cotton, 88" x 72 1/2"
Museum of Our National Heritage Collection
Gift of Mrs. Everett C. Carey

Red and green cotton appliqued onto white muslin. Quilt made up of thirty 14 1/2" squares decorated with appliqued and embroidered symbols within a wreath of leaves. Hearts appliqued in the corners of each block. Each square was assembled and quilted separately and then joined together.

The quilt was made by the members of the Beacon Light Chapter of the Order of Eastern Star and presented to their sponsors, Beacon Light Lodge.

118
CARPET
c. 1860's
Wool, 51 1/2" x 36"
Lent by Mr. and Mrs. Foster McCarl, Jr.

Red and black woven carpeting. Masonic design of arch and pavement, broken column, ark, and other Masonic symbols. Probably used in a Masonic Lodge.

119
MASTER'S CHAIR
1864
Walnut, 62"
Museum of Our National Heritage Collection
Gift of Union Lodge, A.F. & A.M., Dorchester, Massachusetts

This Master's Chair was presented to Union Lodge in 1864 by Brother George Woodman when the Lodge moved to new and larger quarters made necessary because, "The war of Rebellion, which has been in progress for three years, had excited unusual interest in Masonry in the community, and all the Lodges received large additions to their numbers." (*An Historical Sketch of Union Lodge*, Spartan Press, Inc., Boston, 1926, p. 86).

120
CARPET
c. 1881
Wool, 62" x 36"
Lent by Mr. and Mrs. Charles V. Hagler

Red and green woven carpeting taken from a lodge in Tombstone, Arizona. The first lodge in Tombstone was Solomon Lodge, chartered June 14, 1881, and the carpeting was probably part of the original furnishings.

The design is somewhat different from 118. The repeated pattern is bordered by a band of symbols including a triangle, sword, star, and heart. The main design consists of a "G" suspended from a chain above an altar and within an arch. Other symbols include the five orders of architecture, the Bible, square and compasses, moon and stars, winding stairs, pillars and globes, and the plumb, square and level, and mosaic pavement.

118

120

125

121
"THE MASONIC CHART"
Currier & Ives, New York City, N.Y., 1876
Lithograph, comp. 17 1/2" x 13 3/8"
Museum of Our National Heritage Collection
Gift of Eldon T. Urquhart

Colored lithograph based on the Amos Doolittle engraving of "The Master's Carpet" in Jeremy Cross's 1819 edition of *The Masonic Chart*.

122
PITCHER
c. 1850
Ceramic, 5 1/2"
Lent by Mr. and Mrs. Charles V. Hagler

Copper luster pitcher with raised floral designs. Square and compasses and "G" molded in relief on bottom.

123
GOBLET
United States, 1880's
Glass, 5 3/4"
Lent by Mrs. Kenneth Hamilton

Non-flint glass goblet in the "Shrine" pattern (Metz no. 1319). Design includes the crescent moon and five-pointed star.

124
ICE CREAM MOLD
New York, late 19th century
Metal, 6" x 5 1/4"
Museum of Our National Heritage Collection

Hinged mold in the shape of the square and compasses. Marked "E. & Co. N.Y./HAZCO."

125
ICE CREAM MOLD
New York, late 19th century
Metal, 5 1/2" x 5 1/4"
Lent by Mr. and Mrs. Charles V. Hagler

Hinged mold in the shape of a square and compasses with "G" in center. Marked "E. & Co. N.Y."

126
TRIVET
Cast iron, 6 3/4" x 4", c. 1890
Museum of Our National Heritage Collection

Horseshoe shaped trivet with pierced design of square, compasses and "G".

127
TRIVET
Cast iron, 10 1/2" x 4", late 19th century
Lent by Mr. and Mrs. Charles V. Hagler

Flat iron shaped trivet with long handle. Pierced design of heart, pillars and arch, and square and compasses.

128
SHELF
Wood, 21" x 13 1/2", 19th century
Lent by Mr. and Mrs. Charles V. Hagler

Collapsible wooden shelf with pierced design of pillars and arch, square and compasses, winged hourglass, "G" on hinged bracket supporting shelf.

129
MATCH HOLDER
19th century
Wood, 9" x 5 1/2"
Lent by Mr. and Mrs. Charles V. Hagler

Pierced design of square, compasses, and "G" above a shield shaped plaque with two receptacles for matches.

130
LAMP GLOBE
19th century
Glass, 7" x 8" diam.
Lent by Mr. and Mrs. Charles V. Hagler

Frosted lamp globe with symbols of square and compasses, plumb, and level around sides. Probably used in a lodge.

131
CANE
Texas or Mexico, 19th century
Wood, 36"
Museum of Our National Heritage Collection
Gift of Robert S. McKinley

Wooden cane carved with square, compasses and "G", an eagle on a cactus holding a snake, and a snake entwined around the lower part of the cane. Although this cane was found in Davenport, Iowa, on the Mississippi River, the symbol of the eagle holding a serpent identifies it with Mexico. It probably dates from the 1830 to 1848 period of either Texas or Mexico. Austin, Houston, and other prominent Texans were Freemasons, and Freemasonry also played a role in the politics of Mexico in this period. In 1830 the Mexican National Rite was instituted as an offshoot of the two Masonic political factions, the Scottish Rite and York Rite of Mexico. One of the nine degrees of the Mexican National Rite was the Knight of the Mexican Eagle and possibly the cane was associated with that organization (Gould's *History of Freemasonry Throughout the World*, Charles Scribner's Sons, N.Y., 1936, v. IV, p. 108).

132
HOOKED RUG
19th century
Wool, 24" x 36"
Lent by Mr. and Mrs. Charles V. Hagler

Half-circle hooked rug with symbols of square, compasses, and "G", and floral border.

133
SQUARE AND COMPASSES
South Ryegate, Vermont, 1890
Wax, 25 1/4" x 24 1/4"
Museum of Our National Heritage Collection

White wax flowers arranged in shape of the Masonic square, compasses, and "G". Mounted in a gold framed shadow box on black velvet. Made by Mrs. J.F. Whitehill of South Ryegate, Vermont, in 1890.

134
SHELF CLOCK
Seth Thomas, Plymouth, Connecticut, c. 1840-50
Wood, 16 3/8" x 10 3/4" x 3 1/2"
Museum of Our National Heritage Collection

Thirty hour brass movement, mahogany bevel case. Masonic square, compasses, and "G" painted in reverse on glass panel of case.

135
DAGUERREOTYPE CASE
S. Peck & Co., mid-19th century
Thermoplastic, 3 3/4" x 3 3/8"
Museum of Our National Heritage Collection

Black thermoplastic case with molded design of Masonic pillars, arch, eye, square, compasses, and "G" in relief. Label inside reads: "Genuine/Union Case/Improved/Fine Gilt and Burnished/Hinge./S. Peck & Co./Manufacturers."

135

136
BOX
Scovill Manufacturing Co., New York, mid-19th century
Wood and thermoplastic, 3 1/4" x 4 7/8" x 4 7/8"
Museum of Our National Heritage Collection

Small wooden box with brown thermoplastic lid with molded design of Masonic pillars and arch, all-seeing eye, square, compasses, and "G", open Bible, and acanthus leaves. Bottom of box marked "Scovill Mfg. Co. N.Y." The Scovill Co. also made daguerreotype cases.

135

137
HORSE BRASS
19th century
Brass, 3 3/4" x 3"
Museum of Our National Heritage Collection

Horse brass used as decoration on harnesses in the shape of the Masonic square and compasses in serrated circle.

138
PITCHER
19th century
Ceramic, 9 1/2"
Lent by Mr. and Mrs. Charles V. Hagler

Rockingham glaze pitcher with design of Masonic square, compasses, and "G" molded in relief.

139

139
EMBROIDERY
c. 1875
Wool on perforated card, 13" x 25"
Lent by Mr. and Mrs. Charles V. Hagler

Perforated card embroidery in shaded wools, with foil backing. "Trust in God" above an open Bible with the square and compasses and flanked by the Masonic pillars and globes.

140
CORKSCREW
John Hasselbring, Brooklyn, New York, 1906
Silver, 5"
Museum of Our National Heritage Collection

Silver corkscrew that screws into a case engraved with the Masonic square, compasses, "G", and slipper. Initials "J.C.B."

141
SHAVING MUG
Limoges, late 19th century
Ceramic, 3 7/8"
Museum of Our National Heritage Collection

White shaving mug with the name "Chas. A. Foss" and the Masonic square, compasses, and "G" in gold. Marked "T & V" in square, "Limoges."

142
SHAVING MUG
C.T. Altwasser, late 19th century
Ceramic, 3 1/2"
Museum of Our National Heritage Collection

White mug with square, compasses, and "G", and "Masonic" surrounded by wreath of flowers printed in green. Green bands on base, rim, and handle. Marked "C.T. Altwasser."

143
RAZOR
19th century
Steel and horn, 6"
Lent by Supreme Council, Ancient and Accepted Scottish Rite of
  Freemasonry, Southern Jurisdiction

Horn handled razor blade engraved with Masonic symbols and marked "Carson's Superior Razor."

144
WATCH
Dudley Watch Co., Lancaster, Pennsylvania, c. 1922
Silver, 1 3/4" diam.
Museum of Our National Heritage Collection
Gift of Mrs. Willis R. Michael

Masonic watch with bridge plates in the form of the Masonic symbols. This is the earliest model (serial numbers 500-2000) which is distinguished by the fact that the Bible is engraved on the plate.

144

145
WATCH
Dudley Watch Co., Lancaster, Pennsylvania, c. 1923-1925
Gold, 1 3/4" diam.
Museum of Our National Heritage Collection
Gift of Mrs. Willis R. Michael

Masonic watch with bridge plates in the form of Masonic symbols. This is the second model (serial numbers 2001-4800) which is distinguished by the fact that the Bible is applied to the plate and soldered.

After the company's bankruptcy in 1925, the factory and stock was managed by P.W. Baker and Co., J.F. Apple Company, and finally purchased by the X-L Watch Company of New York in 1935. Since then they have continued to produce a limited number of Dudley Watches each year with the unused parts. These later watches can be identified by the fact that the Bible is pinned onto the plate rather than soldered.

144

146
WATCH WINDING KEYS
c. 1850, 1 7/8" and 2 1/4"
Museum of Our National Heritage Collection
Gift of Mrs. Willis R. Michael

Two watch winding keys. One is silver, shaped like a keystone, with the Royal Arch inscription, "HTWSSTKS". The other is gilded brass, with the Masonic arch and columns, level, square, compasses, "G" and ark.

147
LAMP
19th century
Glass and marble, 9"
Lent by Miss Dorothy-Lee Jones

White opaque glass font with marble base. Masonic symbols of ark, pot of incense, anchor, and others painted in gold around the font.

LENDERS TO THE EXHIBITION

Albany Institute of History and Art
Chicago Historical Society
Connecticut Historical Society
Corning Museum of Glass
Mr. Carl Crossman
Essex Institute
Mr. H. Sterling French
Grand Lodge of Massachusetts, A.F. & A.M.
Mr. and Mrs. Charles V. Hagler
Mr. John Hamilton
Mrs. Kenneth Hamilton
Henry Ford Museum
Mr. Mark Hollander
Dr. and Mrs. Oscar Hollander
Mr. D. Roger Howlett
Miss Dorothy-Lee Jones

Lodge of St. Andrew, A.F. & A.M., Boston, Massachusetts
Mr. and Mrs. Gerald Knicely
Mr. Foster McCarl, Jr.
Munson-Williams-Proctor Institute
Mr. Russell Ward Nadeau
New York State Historical Association
Mr. Donald Noble
Old Sturbridge Village
Peabody Museum of Salem
Portland Museum of Art
St. John's Lodge No. 2, A.F. & A.M., Middletown, Connecticut
Sandwich Glass Museum
Supreme Council, Ancient and Accepted Scottish Rite of Freemasonry, Southern Jurisdiction
Washington Lodge, A.F. & A.M., Lexington, Massachusetts
Mr. and Mrs. Fred R. Youngren

BIBLIOGRAPHY

Anderson, M.S., *Europe in the Eighteenth Century, 1713-1783*. New York, Holt, Rinehart and Winston, Inc., 1961.

Arnold, C.L., *The Rationale and Ethics of Freemasonry or the Masonic Institution considered as a means of social and individual progress*. New York, Robert Macoy, 1858.

Boston Museum of Fine Arts, *Paul Revere's Boston*. New York Graphic Society, 1975.

Brown, William Moseley, *From Operative to Speculative*. Masonic Service Association, January 29, 1958.

Carr, Harry, "Guided Tour of Grand Lodge Library and Museum-Freemason's Hall, London". *Transactions of Quatuor Coronati Lodge*, Vol. 78, (London, 1965).

Cassirer, Ernst, *The Philosophy of the Enlightenment*. Boston, Beacon Press, 1955.

Castells, F. de P., *English Freemasonry in its period of transition, A.D. 1600-1700*. London, Rider & Co., 1931.

Coil, Henry Wilson, *Coil's Masonic Encyclopedia*. New York, Macoy Publishing Co., 1961.

Conder, Edward, Jr., *Records of the Hole Crafte & Fellowship of Masons*. London, Swan Sonnenschein & Co., 1894.

Cross, Jeremy, *Masonic Chart*. New Haven, 1819. Engravings by Companion A. Doolittle.

Darrah, Delmar Duane, *History and Evolution of Freemasonry*. Chicago, The Charles T. Powner Co., 1951.

Fay, Bernard, *Revolution and Freemasonry*. Boston, Little Brown and Co., 1935.

Forbes, Harriette Merrifield, *Gravestones of Early New England*. New York, DaCapo Press, 1967.

Gould, Robert Freke, *A Library of Freemasonry*. Philadelphia, John C. Yorston Publishing Co., 1911.

Gowans, Alan, "Freemasonry and the neoclassic style in America." *Antiques*, (February, 1960).

Grand Lodge 1717-1967, United Grand Lodge of England. Oxford, University Press, 1967.

Hammond, William, *Masonic Emblems and Jewels, Treasures at Freemason's Hall—London*. London, George Philip and Son, 1917.

Hardie, James, *The New Free-Mason's Monitor or Masonic Guide*. New York, George Long, 1818.

Hunt, Charles Clyde, *Masonic Symbolism*. Cedar Rapids, Iowa, Laurence Press Co., 1939.

Lanmon, Dwight P., *The Baltimore Glass Trade, 1780-1820*. Charlottesville, Winterthur Portfolio 5, University Press of Virginia, 1969.

Little, Nina Fletcher, *American Decorative Wall Painting, 1700-1850*. New York City, Old Sturbridge Village and Studio Publication, 1952.

BIBLIOGRAPHY

McCauley, Robert H., *Liverpool Transfer Designs on Anglo-American Pottery.* Portland, Southworth Anthoensen Press, 1942.

McClinton, Katherine Morrison, *Collecting American 19th Century Silver.* New York, Scribner's, 1968.

McKearin, George S. & Helen, *American Glass.* New York, Crown Publishers, 1948.

Mastai, Boleslaw, *The Stars and Stripes.* New York, Alfred A. Knopf, 1973.

Mercer, Henry Chapman, *The Bible in Iron.* Doylestown, Pennsylvania, Bucks County Historical Society, 1961.

Mudge, Jean McClure, *Chinese Export Porcelain.* University of Delaware Press, 1962.

New York State Historical Association, *Outward Signs of Inner Beliefs: Symbols of American Patriotism.* Cooperstown, New York, 1975.

Oliver, George, *A Dictionary of Symbolical Masonry.* New York, Jno. W. Leonard and Co., 1855.

Oliver, George, *Historical Landmarks of Freemasonry.* London, 1846.

Pound, Roscoe, *Lectures on the Philosophy of Freemasonry.* Anamosa, Iowa, The National Masonic Research Society, 1915.

Tatsch, J. Hugo, *Freemasonry in the Thirteen Colonies.* New York, Macoy Publishing Co., 1929.

Thorne, Atwood, *Pink Lustre Pottery.* London, B.T. Batsford, 1926

Webb, Thomas Smith, *Freemason's Monitor.* Albany, 1797-1816.

COLOPHON

This book has been typeset, printed and bound by the Pantagraph Printing Company and Illinois Graphics, Inc., both of Bloomington, Illinois. The text was set in 10/14 Univers Medium type created by Adrian Frutiger of Switzerland, and printed on Lustro Offset Enamel Dull paper (80 lb.) manufactured by S. D. Warren Co., U.S.A. The book was designed by Addis M. Osborne.

Two thousand books were paper bound for the Museum of Our National Heritage, Lexington, Massachusetts. A limited edition of nine hundred ninety-nine numbered copies has been hard bound for distribution to members of The Masonic Book Club.

SCOTTISH RITE MASONIC
MUSEUM OF OUR NATIONAL HERITAGE
LEXINGTON, MASSACHUSETTS

Dedicated April 20, 1975

Related Titles from Westphalia Press

Ancient Mysteries and Modern Masonry: The Collected Writings of Jewel P. Lightfoot, Edited by Billy J. Hamilton Jr.

Jewel P. Lightfoot. Former Attorney General of the State of Texas. Past Grand Master of the Masonic Grand Lodge of Texas. From humble beginnings in rural Arkansas, he worked to become an educated man who excelled in law and Freemasonry. He was a gentleman of his time, well-known as a scholar, public speaker, and Masonic philosopher.

Essay on The Mysteries and the True Object of The Brotherhood of Freemasons
by Jason Williams

This isn't a reprint of a classic. It's a new rendition with new life breathed into it, to be enjoyed both by the layperson trying to understand the Craft and Masonic scholars taking a deeper dive into the fraternity's golden years—when the concepts of liberty and equality were still fresh.

Female Emancipation and Masonic Membership:
An Essential Collection
By Guillermo De Los Reyes Heredia

Female Emancipation and Masonic Membership: An Essential Combination is a collection of essays on Freemasonry and gender that promotes a transatlantic discussion of the study of the history of women and Freemasonry and their contribution in different countries.

Freemasonry, Heir to the Enlightenment
by Cécile Révauger

Modern Freemasonry may have mythical roots in Solomon's time but is really the heir to the Enlightenment. Ever since the early eighteenth century freemasons have endeavored to convey the values of the Enlightenment in the cultural, political and religious fields, in Europe, the American colonies and the emerging United States.

Freemasonry: A French View
by Roger Dachez and Alain Bauer

Perhaps one should speak not of Freemasonry but of Freemasonries in the plural. In each country Masonic historiography has developed uniqueness. Two of the best known French Masonic scholars present their own view of the worldwide evolution and challenging mysteries of the fraternity over the centuries.

Worlds of Print: The Moral Imagination of an Informed Citizenry, 1734 to 1839
by John Slifko

John Slifko argues that freemasonry was representative and played an important role in a larger cultural transformation of literacy and helped articulate the moral imagination of an informed democratic citizenry via fast emerging worlds of print.

Why Thirty-Three?: Searching for Masonic Origins
by S. Brent Morris, PhD

What "high degrees" were in the United States before 1830? What were the activities of the Order of the Royal Secret, the precursor of the Scottish Rite? A complex organization with a lengthy pedigree like Freemasonry has many basic foundational questions waiting to be answered, and that's what this book does: answers questions.

The Great Transformation: Scottish Freemasonry 1725-1810
by Dr. Mark C. Wallace

This book examines Scottish Freemasonry in its wider British and European contexts between the years 1725 and 1810. The Enlightenment effectively crafted the modern mason and propelled Freemasonry into a new era marked by growing membership and the creation of the Grand Lodge of Scotland.

Getting the Third Degree: Fraternalism, Freemasonry and History
Edited by Guillermo De Los Reyes and Paul Rich

As this engaging collection demonstrates, the doors being opened on the subject range from art history to political science to anthropology, as well as gender studies, sociology and more. The organizations discussed may insist on secrecy, but the research into them belies that.

A Place in the Lodge: Dr. Rob Morris, Freemasonry and the Order of the Eastern Star
by Nancy Stearns Theiss, PhD

Ridiculed as "petticoat masonry," critics of the Order of the Eastern Star did not deter Rob Morris' goal to establish a Masonic organization that included women as members. Morris carried the ideals of Freemasonry through a despairing time of American history.

Brought to Light: The Mysterious George Washington Masonic Cave
by Jason Williams MD

The George Washington Masonic Cave near Charles Town, West Virginia, contains a signature carving of George Washington dated 1748. This book painstakingly pieces together the chronicled events and real estate archives related to the cavern in order to sort out fact from fiction.

Dudley Wright: Writer, Truthseeker & Freemason
by John Belton

Dudley Wright (1868-1950) was an Englishman and professional journalist who took a universalist approach to the various great Truths of Life. He travelled though many religions in his life and wrote about them all, but was probably most at home with Islam.

History of the Grand Orient of Italy
Emanuela Locci, Editor

No book in Masonic literature upon the history of Italian Freemasonry has been edited in English up to now. This work consists of eight studies, covering a span from the Eighteenth Century to the end of the WWII, tracing through the story, the events and pursuits related to the Grand Orient of Italy.

westphaliapress.org

Policy Studies Organization

The Policy Studies Organization (PSO) is a publisher of academic journals and book series, sponsor of conferences, and producer of programs.

Policy Studies Organization publishes dozens of journals on a range of topics, such as European Policy Analysis, Journal of Elder Studies, Indian Politics & Polity, Journal of Critical Infrastructure Policy, and Popular Culture Review.

Additionally, Policy Studies Organization hosts numerous conferences. These conferences include the Middle East Dialogue, Space Education and Strategic Applications Conference, International Criminology Conference, Dupont Summit on Science, Technology and Environmental Policy, World Conference on Fraternalism, Freemasonry and History, and the Internet Policy & Politics Conference.

For more information on these projects, access videos of past events, and upcoming events, please visit us at:

www.ipsonet.org

www.ingramcontent.com/pod-product-compliance
Lightning Source LLC
Chambersburg PA
CBHW060032040426
42333CB00042B/2315